Mastering Bowling

Dawson Taylor

Contemporary Books, Inc.
Chicago

Library of Congress Cataloging in Publication Data

Taylor, Dawson.
  Mastering bowling.

  Includes index.
  1. Bowling. I. Title.
GV903.T34 1980   794.6   80-68593
ISBN 0-8092-7049-8
ISBN 0-8092-7047-1 (pbk.)

Dedication

This book is respectfully dedicated to all the old bowlers who never die—the great bowlers of the Detroit Athletic Club, the Cleveland Athletic Club, the Buffalo Athletic Club, and the Pittsburgh Athletic Association. Thanks for some wonderful times in my life!

Published by Contemporary Books, Inc.
180 North Michigan Avenue, Chicago, Illinois 60601
Manufactured in the United States of America
Library of Congress Catalog Card Number: 80-68593
International Standard Book Number: 0-8092-7049-8 (cloth)
                                    0-8092-7047-1 (paper)

Published simultaneously in Canada by
Beaverbooks
953 Dillingham Road
Pickering, Ontario L1W 1Z7
Canada

Contents

Foreword

In 1976 I happened to be bowling in a Professional Bowling Association tournament in Miami, Florida, when Dawson Taylor introduced himself to me. At that time he told me that I was "the world's greatest bowler," and that, therefore, I should write a book to make my bowling technique accessible to every bowler. I was aware that Dawson had written an earlier and highly successful book on bowling, *The Secret of Bowling Strikes,* which advocated the use of the "full roller" style of bowling delivery. I believe that there are several different basic bowling methods as well as several different secrets I could disclose concerning my own success in bowling. The result was that Dawson came to my hometown—Tacoma, Washington—and there we recorded many hours of bowling discussion and photographed my bowling delivery and my own secrets to success. Dawson helped me write the resulting book, *Winning Bowling,* which

was published by Contemporary Books, Inc., and has enjoyed excellent sales.

Dawson Taylor has now been asked to write another book, this one aimed at the bowler who achieves higher than average scores and wishes to attain greater proficiency or even stardom as a professional bowler. I know that Dawson Taylor is an avid, discerning student of the sport of bowling. As a member of the Detroit Athletic Club and Detroit Golf Club leagues, he averaged nearly 200 pins for more than ten years. He knows what he is talking about when it comes to bowling and is especially expert in the mental side of bowling. Without reservation, I highly recommend this new book by Dawson Taylor, *Mastering Bowling.* It may make you a champion, too!

Earl Anthony
Tacoma, Washington
1980

Acknowledgments

I would like to express my sincere appreciation to Earl Anthony for his friendship and his counsel. Thanks, too, to my professional bowler models—John Ruggerio of the famous Stroh bowling team and Del Warren, future star of the Professional Bowlers Tour. I thank my nonprofessional bowler models as well: Ethel Larson, Mary Last, Robin Reams, and little Scott Larsen. Credit is also due Bill Taylor, who provided the scientific basis for the discussion of ball balance and ball tracks.

Dawson Taylor

Introduction: So You Want to Be a Master Bowler

The great public acceptance of my earlier bowling instruction book, *Winning Bowling,* written with Earl Anthony, has been most gratifying. We have received many compliments and letters of inquiry from readers, most of whom are serious, dedicated bowlers who wish to attain championship-caliber ability. They asked many questions about the fine points of the bowling game and made me realize that there was a great demand for a bowling instruction book that would truly teach good bowlers how to bowl even better. Such a volume would expose the so-called top-drawer or inside secrets—both physical and mental—of championship bowling.

Let's describe the typical reader this type of book might help. If the description fits you, you can be sure that *Mastering Bowling* is meant for you.

You are either a male bowler who scores 165 to 180 or a female bowler who achieves scores of 145 to 160. You might be carrying an even higher average than these. The important factor, however, is that you want to improve your game and, if possible, become a bowling champion someday. Let's call you a "top bowler" at this time. Eventually, with the help of this book, you can become a champion bowler or a master bowler.

This book offers you, as a top bowler, the opportunity to become a great bowler with a well-rounded style, a champion in your own league—even a champion in the world of professional bowling.

What will you learn through *Mastering Bowling*? The answer is everything you need to know to become a master bowler. Will you be able to learn all the top-drawer tricks of championship bowling? We cannot offer any guarantees; but until you try to learn you will never know whether or not you can fulfill your potential for success as a bowler. Some of the special knowledge you will obtain here may prove difficult for you to put into practice. For example, the trick of changing speed as the lane conditions vary is probably one of the most difficult techniques to learn and carry out successfully. Some bowlers simply cannot learn to change speed and are reconciled to rolling at the same speed all the time, making adjustments by changing their angle of attack. You may be such a bowler. Don't worry. You can still be a master bowler.

Perfecting the game of bowling is like assembling a monstrous jigsaw puzzle. It goes without saying that champion bowlers must have a strong, consistent, well-controlled strike ball. They must be able to make the spare every time. They must acquire such great control over the bowling ball that they can convert a high percentage of their wide-open splits. They must be able

to control their emotions under pressure. They must learn how to practice bowling both on the lanes and in the privacy of their own homes. They must know how to bring both body and mind to the peak of efficiency in order to execute the physical and mental acts of bowling. This book will help you put all these pieces of the puzzle together. Do not be discouraged, however, if you cannot learn and use every trick that is taught in the following pages. Whether or not you ever reach the championship level of bowling, we promise that just knowing what the bowling game is all about will be of great satisfaction to you.

With these words of advice, let us now take you on the road to mastering bowling!

1
The Grip

We will now consider the major elements in developing a fundamental effective bowling style. The first part of the bowling delivery begins with taking the proper grip on the ball as it is held in front of the bowler in the pre-delivery position.

Here is the best way to achieve a consistent grip on the ball. If you are right-handed, hold the ball in your left hand, resting it on the inside of your left forearm. Turn it until the thumb and finger holes are accessible to the fingers of the right hand. If you are left-handed, hold the ball in your right hand and turn it toward the left fingers. Always place your fingers in the holes before you insert your thumb in its hole. After you have put your fingers into the finger holes and positioned each of them against the sides of the holes—giving you the same feel on every grip—lay your gripping hand across the ball and put your thumb all the way into the thumb hole. I suggest that, when your ball driller drills a new ball for you, you should insist that he drill out the bottoms of your finger holes very carefully, almost millimeter by millimeter, so that you can set your fingertips in exactly the same position every time by restricting the depth to which they can be inserted. Also remember that the bottoms of the finger holes must be gently rounded to fit the shape of your fingertips. This is a delicate procedure but one that is well worth the trouble.

Put your thumb all the way into the thumb hole. If there is any room for movement to the side of the hole, it is too big for you. If your skin is pinched or pulled as you snap your thumb out of the hole, it is too small. You should be able to feel the surface of the thumb hole all around your thumb. Here is another rule: if you cannot hold your ball with your thumb alone in the ball, the thumb hole is too big or the ball is too heavy. The weight of the ball is held primarily by the thumb until the moment of release, at which time the ball weight is transferred to the inside of the fingers. The finger holes should not fit as snugly as the thumb hole. If they are too tight, a vacuum effect may result, causing a popping sound as the fingers come out, as well as a drag on the ball. In addition, the fingers may not release in a consistent manner, creating inconsistent ball action, which is most undesirable.

If you find that you are releasing the ball before you want to, or before you expect to, remember that it probably is your thumb that is losing the ball, not the fingers.

Earl Anthony shows how he inserts his fingers into the holes before he puts his thumb into its hole. Anthony rolls a full fingertip ball for greatest effectiveness in striking power.

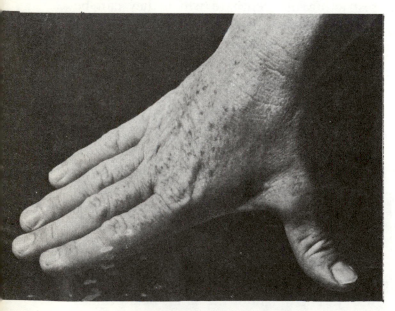

Much of ball drilling depends on the anatomy of the hand. Some individuals have thumbs that angle backward, away from the fingers (reverse pitch) as shown here.

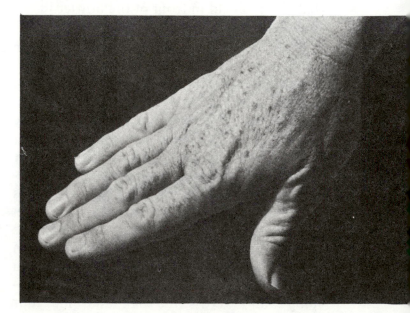

The ball driller must fit each ball to the individual's hand. In this case the thumb angles more toward the fingers than away from them (forward pitch).

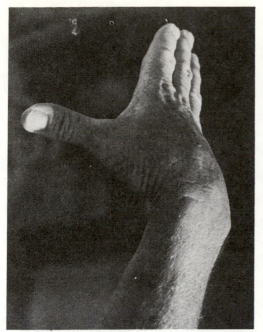 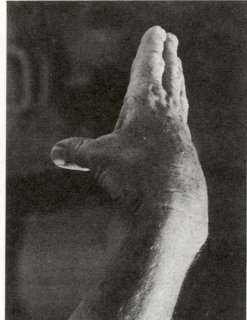 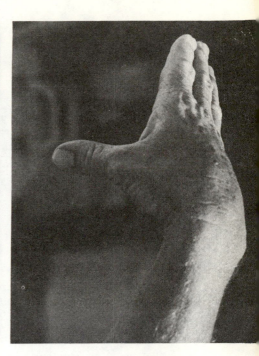

(Upper left): Here is reverse pitch of the thumb from another angle. Excessive reverse pitch in the thumb hole is a true problem-maker for many bowlers. If you have a heavy callus on the top of your thumb, it is nearly always caused by excessive reverse pitch. *(Center):* This photo will give you an idea of what is meant by under-the-palm drilling. Every bowler must find the thumb angle that suits him or her best for easy, quick release of the thumb—without excessive wear or hang-up in the thumb hole. *(Upper right):* This photo illustrates a "normal" thumb angle, neither under the palm nor reverse. The bowler should consult a good ball driller and patiently experiment with many different thumb angles to find the best one. A properly drilled ball is the key to success in bowling.

Here is a trick to help locate your grip the same way every time. You can ask your ball driller to drill you a pinkie spot for the tip of your little finger. If you examine this photo carefully, you will see that the bowler's second and third fingers are in a semifingertip grip and that the little finger fits into its own little depression on the side of the ball.

Del Warren, future star of the professional bowler's tour, uses a ball that is drilled for a fingertip delivery. One of his personal tricks to make sure that his fingers stay outside of the ball during his backswing is to tuck his little finger under on the side of the ball. Many good bowlers use this trick. It puts a strain on the little finger but it helps to standardize your delivery so that you release the ball the same way every time.

2
The Squeeze

There are many secrets to becoming a master bowler, but there is one in particular that every master bowler must have in order to be a champion. It is the secret of putting action into the bowling ball, that is, the spin that causes the ball to hook strongly into the 1-3 strike pocket and gives it enough power to carry through to the 5-pin and cause all ten pins to fall for a strike.

This secret is called by various names—lift, finger-lift, action—but the most descriptive name for it is *the squeeze,* because the action of the fingers in lifting the ball at the delivery point (the foul line) is not unlike the finger action you would use to squeeze a small ball in the palm of your hand, clenching the third and fourth fingers against the palm of the hand. When this finger action is used while the ball is leaving your hand at the foul line, the result is a lift or squeeze on the ball. This squeeze causes the ball to begin to rotate on an axis to the left-hand side of the headpin (for right-handed bowlers). After its initial momentum has carried it about twenty feet down the lane, this action allows the ball to begin to roll on that axis, or to hook in toward the pocket.

The photographs that follow will give you a graphic idea of the squeeze and show you how you can practice the finger action in the privacy of your own home until you can accomplish it on every delivery. Once you have learned the secret of the squeeze, you are on your way to becoming a master bowler.

Here is the secret of master bowling: the bowling ball is squeezed or lifted by the bowler's fingers at the explosion point of the delivery the exact second that the ball passes the sliding foot at the foul line.

Here is the explosion point, with the squeeze or lift being applied to the ball. The ball is lofted out onto the lane, traveling about an inch above the boards for anywhere from six inches to a foot and a half before it will touch down onto the line. Notice that the left foot is still sliding toward its designated dot target on the approach.

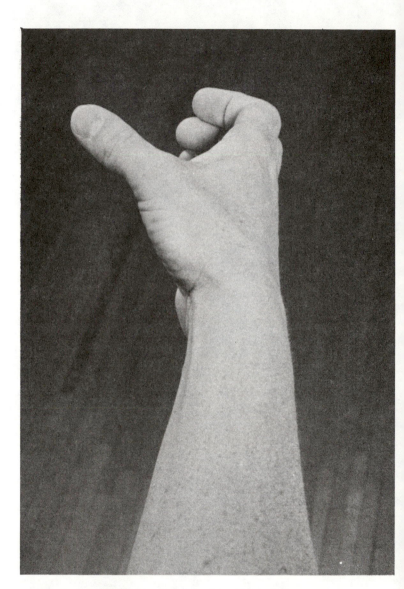

Here is the explosion point of the delivery a fraction of a second after the fingers have imparted their squeezing, lifting action to the ball as it leaves the fingers. The fingers have not yet had time to close completely.

This is a view of the starting hand position without the bowling ball. Note the flat line of the hand and forearm, the thumb pointing inward to the left (in this case to a ten o'clock position). There is tension in the fingers as they prepare to impart the squeeze or lift at the line.

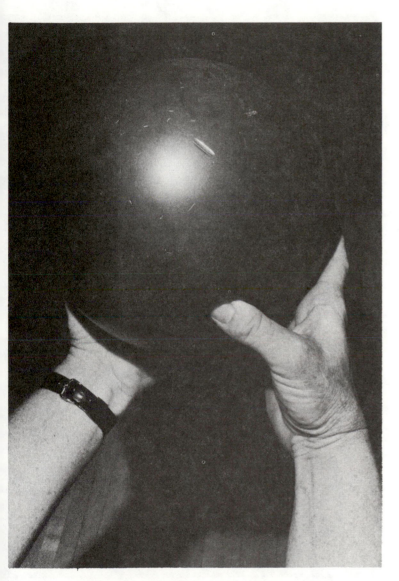

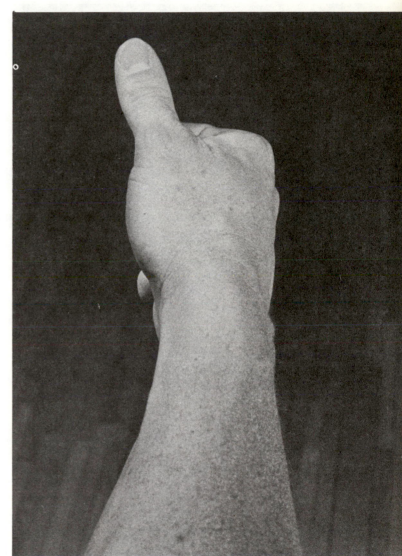

This is the starting position with the bowler about to insert his thumb into the thumb hole. The bowler must visualize his finger position in relation to the clock dial. Here his thumb is pointing to ten o'clock; his other two fingers, inside the ball, are pointing to four o'clock.

Here is a view of the completed squeeze or lift. Notice that the wrist position has not changed, and check the flat line along the back of the hand and up the forearm. The thumb has moved slightly forward to an eleven o'clock position. The thumb is still pointing to the inside of the body, to the left of the headpin.

Here's another view of the beginning hand position. This bowler is going to deliver his ball on a ten o'clock–four o'clock axis and is visualizing the white arrow pointing to ten o'clock. His thumb, inside the ball, should be pointing to the same ten o'clock position as he looks down at the ball. You may use an eleven o'clock–five o'clock axis or any variation in between twelve o'clock and nine o'clock, as long as you use the same axis consistently.

Here the ball has just started to turn as a result of the squeeze or lift. Notice that the bowler's thumb has moved forward to an eleven o'clock position and that the fingers are now clenched tightly together, proving that the squeeze has been successfully carried out by the bowler.

(Upper left): This exercise shows the squeeze or lift action in the delivery of the bowling ball. First, place your ball in front of you near your left foot. Put your fingers only in the finger holes and your thumb on top of the ball. Now close your fingers while they are in this position. You will find that the ball wants to run away from you to your left. The ball has been squeezed or lifted. This is what will happen when you deliver the ball out over the foul line with action. *(Upper right):* Finally, you may place your thumb all the way into the thumb hole as you carry out this exercise. From the beginning of your practice, count the number of times you can make the ball revolve on its axis. You will probably discover that, at first, it is difficult to make it complete one full revolution but that after much practice you can drive it around many times. More and more you will achieve the finger sense of what must be done to squeeze or lift the ball at the explosion point. You will recognize the action when you do it and when you don't do it. *(Lower left):* Here's a close-up view of the action the ball takes when the bowler's fingers squeeze or lift it at the explosion point of the delivery. Note that the hand and the wrist have moved straight forward and upward, that the fingers have closed and squeezed or lifted the ball, imparting the counterclockwise turn to the ball. Note that the arrow is disappearing around the side of the ball, indicating that while the ball is moving straight down the lane, it is turning counterclockwise. *(Lower right):* Now you may begin to put your thumb into the thumb hole. Start by inserting it only partially. Keep the thumb very relaxed. Feel the pressure in the fingers, which are ready to lift or squeeze the ball, and in the thumb, which is prepared to make its exit ahead of time.

3
The Delivery

The four-step approach is the accepted and recommended number of steps to be learned in bowling. While there are other step patterns, the four-step approach is considered the simplest to learn, because it is easier for the bowler to synchronize his swing and foot movements throughout a four-step delivery. It is not necessarily better than the three-step, the five-step, or more step deliveries. It is simpler, more functional, and less apt to cause timing troubles. Once the master bowler has perfected the four-step delivery, he may later on with caution experiment with the other types of delivery.

The first step of the four-step delivery is to take a natural step forward on the right foot at the same instant that the ball is pushed away from the body. On the first step the left hand is still supporting the ball. The mere weight of the ball should send it properly forward and downward into the start of the bowling swing.

On the second step the ball is at the bowler's side and begins to move into the lower portion of the backswing as the left foot touches the floor in the approach to the line. The arm is held close to the body and the left arm instinctively starts to seek a natural balancing position without any help from the bowler.

The ball reaches the top of the backswing toward the end of the third step. Momentum is increasing, and the arm is still straight, swinging freely from the shoulder. The first two steps and the movement of the body supply the necessary acceleration. At the end of the third step the ball should be at the peak of the backswing—never higher than the shoulder—and the shoulder should be parallel to the foul line. The downward movement of the ball starts easily and the knees begin to bend, lowering the bowler's body to prepare for the final step on the left foot. This last step is a long slide that generally ends an inch or two in front of the foul line. As long as you maintain consistency, this distance from the foul line may vary a few inches without problems. However,

(Upper left): This is the moment of the pushaway. At the *exact* instant you push the ball forward into its arc, your right foot moves into its first step. If these actions are timed to coincide precisely, 90 percent of your troubles in timing are over. *(Upper right):* Here is the second step. The ball is dropping into the backswing and the right foot is making its move straight down the imaginary line. Notice that the hand position has not been changed in relation to the body since the pushaway. In orthodox bowling it will not change throughout the entire bowling swing. *(Lower left):* John Ruggerio is at the end of his second step as the ball passes his side. Note his intense concentration on the line he intends to use. Note, too, his excellent balance with his left arm starting to extend naturally to the side to counterbalance the weight of the ball. *(Lower right):* John is starting the final move to the explosion point of his delivery. Note that his fingers are at a six o'clock position in the ball, his thumb at twelve o'clock. His body is now lower and his left knee is bending.

your lateral position should remain constant; that is, you should not be at the center of the lane one time and more to one side at another time.

On the fourth step the knee is bent and you slide on your left foot. Your heel strikes the surface of the lane as your knee straightens out, and the rubber heel of your shoe acts as a brake to stop you at the line. The ball and the left foot should reach the foul line at the same time. The body bends forward in delivering the ball over the foul line. There is a distinct sense of having followed through with the right arm and shoulder as the ball leaves your hand. The ball can be delivered naturally—without any attempt on your part to twist your wrist at the moment of delivery—or you may aid the delivery with what is called a *lift* or *turn*. The fingers of your hand close as the ball

John Ruggiero demonstrates the proper way to apply wrist turn at the explosion point of the delivery. Note that John's fingers are behind the ball just before the release, his thumb just beginning to come out of the ball.

Here is John's delivery a fraction of a second after the preceeding photo. Note that his hand and wrist have turned counterclockwise to impart wrist turn to the ball. At the same time the fingers have squeezed or lifted the ball as well.

leaves the hand, with the thumb coming out of its hole first. With a squeezing, finger snapping, lifting motion of the two fingers that have remained in the ball, the ball is given a rotating momentum which it carries a distance down the lane until its skidding momentum ends and the hooking action begins.

There is no essential difference between the four-step delivery and the five-step delivery. Basically, the five-step delivery is a four-step delivery with the ball carried on the first step. The timing of both deliveries is the same once the four-step ball-pushaway action begins. Some bowlers prefer the five-step delivery because it feels more natural for them to start on the left foot. The five-step delivery also helps if your strides are too long. Necessarily you must shorten your steps or go over the foul

 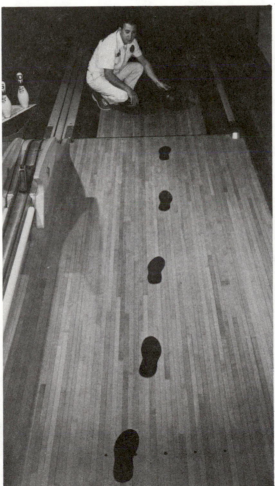 

(Left): Here is an example of an effective, smooth delivery with excellent form at the line. Note the squareness of the hip line to the foul line, the follow-through with the right shoulder, the sense of staying down at the line, and the balance shown by the extended left arm. Note that the bowler's head has also stayed down, watching his spot out on the lane. *(Center):* John Ruggiero shows the footwork required to bowl the inside angle. *(Right):* John Ruggiero demonstrates the inside angle, which is bowled from the left side of the center line out toward the 3-pin. This is the customary line for the bowler who uses a lot of wrist turn at the delivery point.

This photo illustrates bowling the inside angle, that is, bowling a line that starts somewhere near the center of the lane and goes out to the right anywhere from one board to several boards. The ball then comes back into the pocket as a result of the action on the ball. This shot was made from the Twenty Board out over the Fifteen Board, which is the number of the board at the third arrow from the right. Good bowlers call the boards by their numbers and always know exactly where they are putting the ball down to start its track and where they are aiming at the break of the boards where the arrows are. Note that the body of the bowler is square to the line of travel and that the follow-through is made directly down the same line.

John Ruggiero demonstrates bowling the outside angle as he bowls over the first arrow. This line is used on extremely stiff lanes, and the bowler's ball usually has a moderate hook. It is a very effective line if the bowler can hold the ball in the pocket and not hit too high on the headpin.

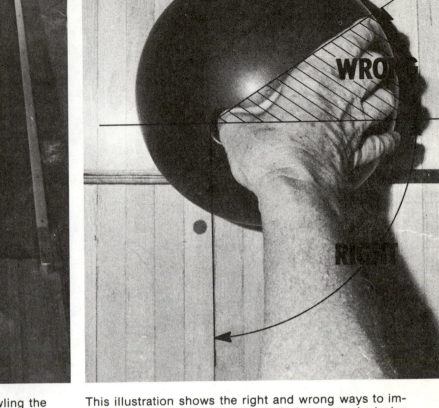

This illustration shows the right and wrong ways to impart wrist turn to the bowling ball. A counterclockwise movement of the fingers from six o'clock to as far as three o'clock will work, but the moment the hand passes the three o'clock point the ball loses action and has been turned too much.

line. The bowler who prefers a faster approach finds the five-step delivery more suitable.

There are other variations on delivery, but the master bowler should concentrate on the orthodox delivery styles.

In the four-step delivery your weight starts out on the left foot; it is transferred to your right foot as you step forward with the right. In the five-step delivery, the reverse is true, of course, with the weight starting out on the right side and then transferring to the left as the left takes the first of the five steps. You should have the feeling that your body is moderately erect throughout your approach to the foul line. Actually, it starts to lean forward midway in the delivery as the ball forces the body downward when the arm goes backward for the backswing.

At the same time that you shift your

(Left): Del Warren and Dawson Taylor discuss the significance of the mental clock. The position shown represents Del's normal finger position at delivery. His fingers are at the five o'clock spot and his thumb is at the eleven o'clock spot, lifting or squeezing the ball forward on that axis. *(Right):* Del Warren demonstrates intense concentration at the line as he delivers this ball. Notice that his head stays down at the line, his right foot slides straight toward his target at the line, his body is balanced beautifully as his left leg swings around his body, and his left arm is extended in counterbalance. Note, too, his unbroken wrist and his fingers closing in the squeeze.

weight forward onto the foot that is taking the first of the last four steps to the line, push the ball away from your body until your arms are fully extended in front of you. You do not want to lift the ball upward from its original position in your stance, nor do you want to drop it prematurely into its downswing. As both arms reach the fully extended position, the left hand smoothly lets the right hand take care of the problem of what to do with the ball. It is as if the left hand is offering the ball to the right hand, saying, "All right, now it's your turn."

When you push the ball straight out from your starting position at waist level, the ball will be in front of you, ready to swing from a height sufficient to give it good momentum. This start of your pushaway should be as free and unrestricted as possible. Try not to muscle the ball or limit its swing in any way. In other words, let the ball do the work it is intended to do. You are going to act as the intermediary that lets it proceed through its backswing, stop at the top of the backswing, and proceed through the downswing and explosion point at the line.

When I stated that you should start the ball at waist level, I merely suggest that you try this method of starting your delivery first. Many excellent bowlers use this method of waist-high pushaway, and one cannot argue with their success. But we will also

Del Warren demonstrates perfect form as he delivers this ball out over the foul line. Note that he has used the inside angle because his sliding foot can be seen approaching the dot five boards to the left of the center of the lane. Note his straight follow-through, the excellent concentration on his target line out on the lane, and the beautiful balance of his body.

Del Warren demonstrates the turned sliding foot at the moment of delivery. This counterclockwise move of the sliding foot puts the bowler farther under the ball and increases his leverage on the ball. It is a difficult trick to do and takes a great deal of practice. However, if you can accomplish it, the results in greater striking power are well worth the effort.

examine some alternatives—for example, the chest-high dropaway or the tentative low-swing start used by Marshall Holman and others.

Once your right heel has accepted your body weight and started you on your straight-ahead footwork toward the line, and your ball reaches its fully extended position at the end of your outstretched right hand, you are committed to that swing. Any error you make at this point will affect the ball swing. That is why it is so important for you to develop and perfect a consistent pushaway in which your arm not only extends the same distance in front of your body every time but it also creates the same angle with the front of your body.

It is obvious that if you push the ball out to belt height on one delivery, to an inch below belt height on the next, and then to an inch above belt height on a third successive delivery, you are adding a variation to

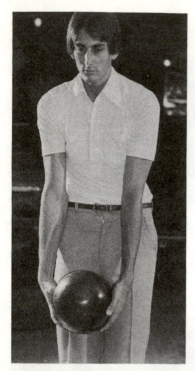

(Left): Del Warren demonstrates another variation of the starting position. Some bowlers, particularly tall ones, like to suspend the ball at the end of the bowling arm with part of its weight supported by the other arm. The ball is held close to the body until the bowler gives it a push away from him and starts it into its forward arc. *(Right):* Del Warren demonstrates another starting position frequently used by the master bowler. The ball is held out in front of the bowler's right side so that it can drop away into the backswing without encountering any interference from the body. The other hand is used to help support the weight of the ball until the delivery begins. Del has his thumb in an eleven o'clock position and his fingers at five o'clock as he starts. He rolls a full spinner with a great deal of wrist turn at the explosion point.

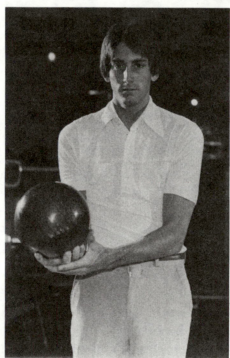

(Left): Del Warren demonstrates another variation of his starting position. Here the ball is held tightly against his body with his left hand helping support the weight of it until the last moment. He keeps the ball well over to his right side so that it can move into its pendulum swing without any interference from the body. *(Center):* Del Warren demonstrates his own personal preference for starting position with the ball. He holds it slightly away from his body, not tightly against it, with his right hand under the ball and his left giving support to the weight of the ball. The ball is on the right side of his body, ready to move forward directly down the line he has chosen as his target line. *(Right):* Here Del Warren demonstrates the necessity of bending forward at the foul line. If the body remains too erect, the movement of the right arm in the backswing is restricted and cramped. With the body of the bowler leaning forward, the backswing is unrestricted and free.

your bowling swing that will lead to inconsistent timing at the foul line. It is essential that you have the physical ability to do something with the ball just when it reaches the bottom of its arc at the foul line; any inconsistency hinders this ability.

Try not to vary the way you start the ball in motion on your first step. If you habitually hold it in front of you at belt height, check yourself on every delivery to see that you are holding it at this height—no higher and no lower—and that your arm is extended precisely the same distance from your body every time.

If, as you bowl, you discover that you need more or less speed on the ball, then and only then should you change the way you start the ball in motion. Of course, you can and should experiment in practice by trying the ball an inch or so higher or lower at the start, with your arm more or less extended from your body, but once you have chosen an exact method, try not to vary it. Keep it exactly the same and you

This photo shows how important it is that the knee of the bowler remain bent as the ball is being delivered over the line. The brake on the heel of the sliding foot must not come down prematurely and abruptly halt the smooth slide to the finish.

This photo illustrates the braking effect of the sliding foot as it reaches the line. When the knee is allowed to straighten prematurely, the heel of the shoe comes down and the rubber sole acts as a sudden brake on the body's forward motion. It is most important that you keep your sliding knee bent as you reach the delivery point of your swing.

will send yourself on the way to consistency.

The squeeze, or lift, of the bowling ball may be accompanied by what is called *turn* or *wrist turn*. Basically, there are two styles of bowling delivery: those with no wrist turn at the explosion point and those with wrist turn at the explosion point.

The bowler who releases the ball with no wrist turn merely keeps the wrist in the same position throughout the backswing and forward swing, with the thumb on the inside of the ball (toward the body). Then, with no effort to rotate the wrist in a counterclockwise fashion, he or she merely lets the ball come off the hand naturally, releasing the thumb first because it is shorter than the rest of the fingers. At the last second of the release, the bowler imparts the squeeze or lift to the ball just as it finally leaves the fingers.

Here is an example of a delivery that would have no action or finger lift on the ball. Note that the fingers have remained relaxed and have not squeezed the ball. This delivery will result in a straight ball that rolls end over end and has no hook, no power at the strike pocket. If the hand and wrist turn the least bit counterclockwise at the delivery, the ball will have a reverse spin and be a "backup" ball, which is very undesirable.

In this mock delivery Del Warren demonstrates several important points. The thumb should remain on the inside as the backswing is taken, the knee must be bent for a proper slide at the line, and the sliding foot must slide straight forward as it reaches the foul line. He is also showing marvelous balance.

The bowler who employs wrist turn releases the ball after a distinct turn of the wrist from, say, a six o'clock to three o'clock finger position. The thumb moves inside the ball from twelve o'clock to ten o'clock (on the way to nine o'clock but never quite reaching it), at which point the thumb pulls out of the ball and allows the fingers to impart the squeeze or lift from a three o'clock to a nine o'clock position.

If the thumb passes nine o'clock on its way from twelve o'clock, the ball has been turned too much and will have poor action.

The bowler who uses wrist turn on the delivery must be careful to use it in the same way every time. That means that you will not be consistent if you release the ball with a turn from six o'clock to four o'clock one time and from six o'clock to three o'clock another time.

The master bowler must decide which delivery method to use according to which one feels most natural. Once you decide on the wrist-turn method, you must concentrate on consistently using the same hand, wrist, and finger action every time.

Del Warren and Dawson Taylor discuss the use of the mental clock to visualize thumb and finger positions at the explosion point. The nine o'clock to three o'clock position shown here would indicate a powerful spinner ball delivered with the thumb pointing to nine o'clock, the fingers squeezing or lifting the ball from the three o'clock side toward the left.

Del Warren demonstrates the footwork of the five-step delivery, which he happens to favor. He holds the ball to his right side with the left hand supporting its weight until the last moment. He takes his first step with his left foot, still carrying the ball, and then pushes the ball forward with his second step. The two movements—the second step and the pushaway—coincide exactly and give him precise timing at the line.

4
Balance

It is obvious to most bowlers, especially early in their careers, that that sixteen-pound ball sometimes acts in a devilish fashion that will throw a bowler off balance. And the more you observe the good bowlers you see that none of them allows the ball to get very far from the body. Some bowlers even exaggerate how close they carry the ball to the right side of the body while remaining very upright in vertical fashion all through the approach and delivery. An upright posture does tend to keep the arm and ball close to the side of the body. If it can be achieved along with a full, smooth delivery, it might be your answer to the problem of imbalance. On the other hand, if it feels unnatural to you to be extremely erect, then allow the ball and your arm to find a groove slightly away from your body but as close to it as your musculature and body movements will allow. Definitely do not allow the right arm to get away from the body any more than you have to; otherwise, you will find yourself suffering a loss of balance at the delivery. Thus the ball may

end up careening from right to left across your body, missing the headpin to the left.

Do not bend to the left, the right, or too far forward. As the ball goes into its backswing, your upper body naturally tilts forward and accepts the tension of the right arm muscles on the backswing. In fact, this forward lean must take place, or else the backswing will be cramped and unnatural.

There is an old adage in bowling that your nose should never pass in front of your knees. This is a good rule to observe. You do not want to bend forward during your slide and release.

Slide by bending your left knee, keeping it bent, and remembering to try to keep your upper body erect. This erect, square-to-the-line approach allows your entire body to stay with the ball and to follow it with your arm a little longer. In addition, it often allows you to impart a little more snap to the release than usual, giving the ball extra power that shows up at the pocket in more action.

5
Ball Fit

To become a master bowler it is necessary for you to have a bowling ball that not only fits your hand "like a glove" but that also fits your bowling style. That is, your ball must have the balance that allows properly timed explosive action toward the strike pocket—not too soon and not too late.

We will first consider the problem of acquiring a bowling ball that is properly fitted for you. Once you have the specifications of that ball, it is relatively easy to apply the same drillings, spans, pitches, finger adjustments and finger depths to a second ball, a third ball, and to as many bowling balls as you need.

I recall an interesting story Earl Anthony told me when we were discussing ball balance for our earlier book. He had been bowling in a tournament in Wisconsin, and during the practice session and pro-amateur tournament he realized that the bowling balls he had with him were simply not working on the conditions of the lanes in Wisconsin. He remembered that back home

in Tacoma he had one particular ball—he called it Number 27—which he felt would work better for him. But could he get the ball in time? He phoned his wife and told her to get that ball and put in on a plane as fast as she could. She did, and most fortunately for Earl, the ball not only arrived in time for him to use it but, most happily, he won the tournament with it!

Bill Taylor of Anaheim, California, the outstanding authority on the subject, has spent almost his entire life studying the problem of ball fitting and has counseled nearly all of the country's top bowlers on their ball balance and ball fitting problems. According to Taylor, twelve individual measurements must be taken into consideration in drilling and preparing a properly fitted bowling ball. Some of these measurements are so technical that we will not discuss them here. However, we will consider the major ones and attempt to give you enough information about ball drilling to know that you can't know it all. You will just have to trust the best ball driller you can find to help you obtain the bowling ball that fits you.

First of all, although we said that your ball should fit like a glove, that description should not necessarily be taken literally. It is possible that, even when your ball fits like a glove and therefore feels good to your hand and fingers, you might release it improperly. You might be forced to squeeze the span to avoid dropping the ball at the line. In general, however, you do want to find a ball that fits your hand well, one that you feel you can handle and control without dropping it.

The most important measurement on a bowling ball is the thumb hole. If the thumb hole is drilled and fitted improperly for you, your thumb will release either too soon or too late. If it releases too soon, you will have one or more of the following problems at the delivery point of the bowling swing:

1. You will drop the ball short of the line.
2. You will be unable to apply proper lift with your fingers.
3. You will pull up short on your slide to the line.
4. You will drop your shoulder at the line.
5. You will be forced to squeeze the ball in order to hang on to it and thus deliver it in inconsistent fashion, hanging on to it one time and not hanging on to it the next.

If your thumb comes out too late in the delivery, there is less time between that instant of thumb exit and the time when your fingers execute the lift. In an effort to compensate, you might find yourself concentrating on what your thumb is doing and not on your target and target line. The result is disturbed aim and bowling inconsistency.

Let us say that you have found the best ball driller in your area and have arranged to have him drill your new bowling ball. He will have an interesting ball-fitting device that has many sizes and pitches for various finger holes. Your thumb will be measured first because it is the most important of the three finger holes to be drilled.

An excellent rule to follow at the start is to have your thumb hole drilled $3/64$ inch larger than the smallest hole your thumb will enter and exit without forcing it in or out of the hole. There should be no drag, just easy entrance and exit. Ask the ball driller not to make the hole too large at the start of the ball-drilling process. Let him know that you want to begin with a snug thumb hole and gradually enlarge it to allow the exact ease of exit you want. It may be necessary for you to return to the driller several times to obtain this kind of fit, but it is well worth the effort. Obviously, once the thumb hole is enlarged too much, it is most difficult, if not impossible, to return to a smaller size. (Note that your ball can always be plugged by having a section cut out of it and replaced with new material, and then redrilling it to other specifications. This is a nuisance and rarely provides a satisfactory solution for the bowler.)

To determine whether or not your ball fits your hand, first check your thumb fit, since it is most important. Here's how to test your thumb fit. Put your thumb all the way into the thumb hole. If there is room for any sideways movement, the hole is too big for you. If your thumb skin is pinched or pulled as you snap your thumb out of the hole, the hole is too small for you. You should be able to feel the surface of the thumb hole all around your thumb when you have it inserted fully into the hole.

Here is another good rule to follow in trying to determine whether or not you have a good thumb fit. If you cannot hold your bowling ball with just your thumb in the ball, the thumb hole is too large for you or the ball is too heavy. The weight of the ball is held primarily by the thumb until the moment of release, at which time the weight of the ball is transferred to the inside of the fingers. The finger holes, on the other hand, should not be fit so tightly. If the finger holes are too tight, a vacuum effect may result, evidenced by a popping sound as the fingers come out; the result will be a drag on the ball rather than the free release you always seek. When the finger holes are too tight, the finger release will be inconsistent, leading to inconsistent ball action.

If you find that you are losing the ball before you want to release it or before you expect to, remember that the culprit will be your thumb hole, not the finger hole.

If your ball is too heavy, you may find that you have difficulty controlling it, preventing you from mastering the way it rolls. Your ability to aim the ball will decrease. You will miss your target more often, and therefore you will miss more spares and strike pockets then you would if you controlled it better. However, if you have a ball that is too light, you may be inclined to try to use too much control, aiming the ball too strongly and bowling less freely than you should; again, you will find yourself missing spares and missing the strike pocket. So, it is obvious that somewhere you have to make a compromise between a light and a heavy ball. Knowing what may or may not happen when you use each kind will help you make up your mind. Oddly enough, it appears that the lighter ball knocks down more spares than does the heavy one; being lighter, it deflects more as it hits the first pin of a multiple-pin spare and so covers more ground as it goes through the pins, thus converting more spares.

6

How to Adjust to Various Lane Conditions

Many different lane conditions affect the way your ball reacts on the surface. Some of the surface materials add resistance to the ball so that it curves broadly. Other materials such as oil cause the ball to slide and lose traction.

Basically, there are three general types of lane conditions: the so-called normal lanes, the running or hooking lanes, and the stiff or nonrunning lanes. Of course, there are hundreds of variations in between these general designations.

The normal lane is one that causes your ball to react the way it does 75 to 90 percent of the time. Let us say that you are accustomed to rolling a ball at medium speed over the second arrow and seeing it move one foot left of the end of the ball track into the 1–3 pocket. For you, a lane that lets your ball react that way is a normal lane.

The running or hooking lanes cause your ball to hook too much. Your ball comes high on the headpin instead of into the pocket. It may even cross over into the

"Brooklyn" pocket, the 1–2. Running lanes are ones that have not been conditioned recently or have been used a great deal without cleaning and surface preparation.

The stiff or nonrunning lanes are those that do not allow your ball to hook much. They have recently been conditioned and often are wet and oily. The ball is unable to grip the surface in its usual manner and slides instead of driving into the pocket.

There are several ways to adjust to various lane conditions, some more easy to effect than others. The most common way to adjust is to change your approach position, keeping the same target or line at the back of the boards. That means that if the lane is running, your first adjustment would be to move your starting position one board left of your normal spot. The reverse procedure would be carried out if you found the lanes stiff—one board to the right at the start, keeping the same target line. Your adjustment may, and often will, be greater than one board to the right or left, but you should make changes gradually to avoid becoming hopelessly confused. Always note exactly where you are placing your aiming foot and which line you are hitting as you roll the ball.

Second, you can make target changes to correct your aim at the pocket. For hooking lanes, you will move your target at the break of the boards to the right, or the outside. Move it to the left or inside for stiff lanes.

Third, you may adjust the distance your ball travels on the lane by setting it down farther out on the lanes or closer to the foul line. Obviously, the farther the ball travels on the lane, the more the lane friction works to help it hook at the end. On a hooking lane the ball must skid farther; on a stiff lane it must skid less.

The speed of your ball affects the length of time the ball has to react to the lane conditions. More speed reduces the hook; less speed increases it. However, speed adjustment is one of the most difficult for any bowler to make. It requires a change in the rhythm of the footwork, and the result is often that the bowler reaches the lane either too soon or too late for a suitably effective delivery. If you hold the ball higher in your stance, you can increase its speed; lower it, and you will reduce its speed. You can use a higher backswing to increase speed, a lower backswing to reduce it. But I warn you, it takes a great deal of practice to be able to increase or decrease ball speed without disturbing the general rhythm of delivery.

Another way to adjust to lane conditions is to use a bowling ball that is harder or softer than usual. A softer ball will grip the surface better than one with a hard surface. So when you encounter hooking lanes, use a harder ball. When you hit stiff lanes, use a softer ball. The master bowler will have many bowling balls and will be familiar with the way each acts on various surfaces.

The basic rule for adjustments to lane conditions is "follow the ball." That means that if your ball is hooking too far left, move left. If it is not hooking enough, move right. Furthermore, don't wait to make adjustments. After you have checked to make sure you are rolling your normal ball, make the move at once so that you don't lose precious time to score.

7
The Dynamics of Bowling Ball Action

In order to be successful, you must send the bowling ball down the lane on a particular path.

The bowling ball must roll down the right-hand side of the lane to a crucial spot a few feet from the pins. It must then hook sharply to the left and clip the front pin, the 1-pin, and the pin just behind it, the 3-pin, in such a precise way that the front pin will knock down the three pins on the left-hand side of the triangle of pins. Meanwhile, the ball continues rolling with power into the remaining three pins—the center one, which is the so-called king pin of the group, and the two behind it—to topple them, too. If a bowler sends a ball straight down the lane into the 1–3 pocket, or the 1–2 pocket for the left-hander, without a quick turn being incorporated into the trajectory, the neat sequence of falling dominoes will take place only infrequently.

No master bowler, professional or amateur, rolls a straight ball. They all throw a hook or at least use some semblance of a curve on the ball.

The bowling ball normally skids after it first touches down on the lane beyond the foul line, then it hooks left, and finally it rolls straight ahead along the line that the hooking action has determined. The normal pattern of skid-hook-roll is 20 feet, 20 feet, and 20 feet successively. So, when you find the ball going into its roll too soon and therefore hitting high on the headpin, you must adjust by placing the ball farther out on the lane. In that way you postpone the moment when the hook ends and the forward roll starts. The reverse is true, too, when the ball is not coming up to the pocket soon enough. You must start the ball closer to the foul line than usual, causing the hooking action to take place sooner and sending the ball into the pocket on time.

There is a happy medium you can aim for in the amount of speed needed for maximum action. An excessively slow ball is just as ineffective as the ball that is too fast. The slow ball causes the action to occur too soon; the fast ball, too late or not at all. Unless your ball is obviously too fast or too slow, try to work out a normal medium speed for yourself and adjust the hitting-the-pocket problem through changes and variation in your stance, your pushaway, your approach, and your target line.

UNDERSTANDING ANGLE

It is very important that the bowler understand the meaning and use of angle in knocking down the pins. The angle is the direction of the bowling ball as it enters the 1–3 pocket on the way to the 5-pin, which is the key, or the kingpin, of the group. If you draw an imaginary line from the right-hand corner of a lane to the 5-pin, you will understand that the angle of entry of the line would be the correct angle to carry a strike. When bowlers discuss angle, they refer only to the last few feet of travel by the ball just before it crashes into the pocket. Therefore, it follows that if your bowling ball has a large hook at the end of its travel, it is necessary for you to deliver the ball at the start of its trip down the lane at a point

somewhere near the center of the lane so that it can roll out to the right, then start to hook, and finally enter the pocket at the angle you need in order to carry a strike.

It is necessary to understand how the ball track affects angle, too. The bowling ball is 27 inches in circumference and about 9 inches wide at its equator. The center of a bowling pin is 4.7666 inches wide. So, if you add the width of the bowling pin to the width of the ball, doubled (remember, it can knock down the pin from either side), it is evident that the bowling track is nearly 23 inches.

The bowling ball is also subject to deflection as it strikes the pins. Go back into the pits sometime and watch what happens when the bowling ball strikes the pins. It bounces one way and another as its 16-pound weight is affected by the 3½-pound weight of the pins. The ball must strike a pin precisely head-on to avoid being deflected by it. Hit a pin on its side and the ball will move to that side. That is one of

This is the full setup of ten pins. The 5-pin is directly behind the headpin. It is the king pin or key to carrying a strike on the first ball bowled. The pins are numbered in sequence starting with the 1-pin, the headpin. The 2-pin and 3-pin are in the second row; the 4-pin, 5-pin, and 6-pin are in the third row; the 7-pin, 8-pin, 9-pin, and 10-pin are in the last row.

the reasons that tandem spares are so difficult to convert. Tandem spares are those in which one pin stands directly behind the other.

You must learn to watch the angle your ball takes in entering the strike pocket. You will learn that, if you frequently leave the 5-pin, you need a greater angle to bring the ball farther in from the side to get to the 5-pin. Master bowlers are always aware of their bowling angle. You must be, too.

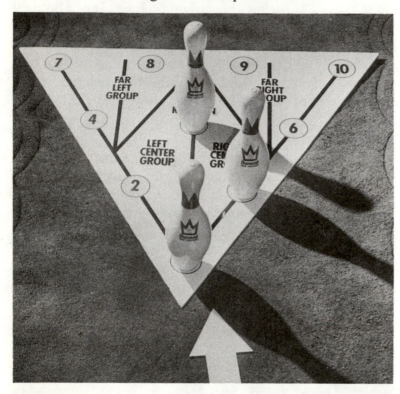

This photograph illustrates high-hard angle on the headpin and 1–3 strike pocket. High-hard angle means the conscious effort on the part of the bowler to counteract running lane conditions by speeding up his ball, cutting down on the amount of final hook at the pocket and hitting higher than usual on the headpins, thus increasing the chance of the ball getting to the 5-pin and not deflecting away from it. It is probably the most effective angle of all because the 5-pin is taken out most directly by the ball itself. This is the angle that is used by most bowlers who do not roll an extrastrong hooking first ball.

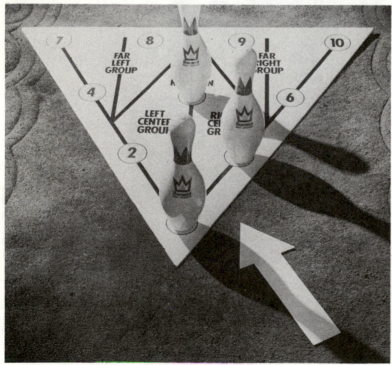

This is an illustration of the strike angle used by the bowler who rolls a strong hook, one that moves across a number of boards at its finish. It is a very effective ball because it gets in behind the headpin, does not waste much of its force in getting the headpin out, and then gets the 5-pin out. It is a real mixer and causes a lot of pin action.

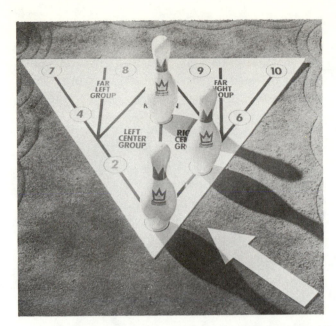
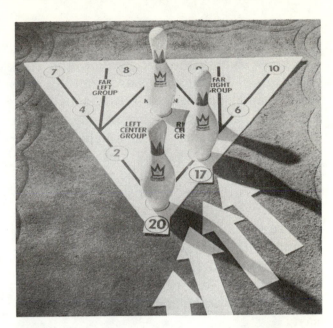

(Left): This photo shows the extremely deep angle used by the very strong bowler, such as Mark Roth. It is a devastating angle, provided the headpin is taken out first. The bowler who uses this angle usually bowls from deep inside, rolls the ball well out toward the channel, and then lets it come in from the right. It is a difficult shot to use and requires a great deal of practice. If you can do it, it is well worth the effort. *(Right):* This photo illustrates the many different angles the bowling ball may take in making a strike. The numbers indicate the board on which the headpin and the 3-pin stand and key in with the boards that the bowler uses to establish the starting position and target at the break of the boards.

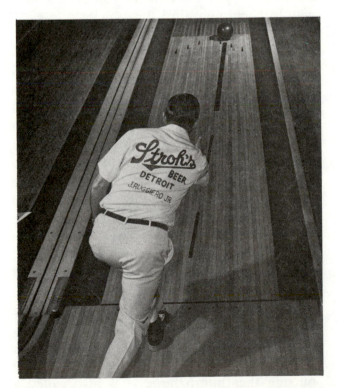

(Left): John Ruggiero demonstrates a strike ball from the inside angle over the thirteenth board between the second and third arrows. This is a customary line for a ball rolled with wrist turn. *(Right):* John Ruggiero demonstrates bowling from the deep inside angle, from the far left starting position over the twenty-second board at the darts. This ball must go out toward the 3-6 pocket and then hook back into the 1-3 pocket. It is a dangerous shot because it requires so much power in the ball to get back to the pocket.

BALL BALANCE

Under the rules of the American Bowling Congress (ABC), the size, weight, and construction of bowling balls are carefully controlled and specified. A bowling ball may not have a circumference of more than twenty-seven inches or a weight of more than sixteen pounds. The rules also provide that "bowling balls shall be so constructed that no less than six sides shall be in proper balance."

Here is the interesting feature of that rule: "proper balance." Apparently the ABC rulemakers realized that no bowling ball could be in perfect balance and allowed some tolerances for imbalance. The rules go on to say,

The following tolerances shall be permissible in the balance of a bowling ball:

10 pounds or more—
a. Not more than 3 ounces difference between top of ball (finger hole side) and the bottom (solid side opposite finger holes)
b. Not more than 1 ounce difference between the sides to the right and left of the finger holes or between the sides in front and back of the finger holes.

Note: The rules go on to provide for weights and balances of balls that are less than ten pounds, but since the master bowler will never use the light ball, we will not discuss them here.

As time went on and bowlers used balls with differing imbalances, it became clear that some effects of imbalance caused more action at the strike pocket than others. When the balance was improper, the ball sometimes actually dived to the right at the end of its track instead of hitting into the pocket.

So, depending on the way your ball rolls, the speed with which you roll it, and the amount of hook you are able to impart to it, the balance of your ball is very important in attaining strike action.

Earl Anthony rolls a semiroller ball. Here are the balances of the three types of balls he normally uses in tournaments. He calls them his strong, stronger, and strongest ball balances.

Strong   ½-ounce side weight
             1-ounce top weight

Stronger ½-ounce side weight
             ½-ounce finger weight
             1½-ounce top weight

Strongest 1-ounce side weight
             1-ounce finger weight
             2½-ounce top weight

You must find out for yourself the best possible balances for your own strong, stronger, and strongest balls. You should consult the best ball driller in your vicinity and work with him to determine those balances. Once you have them, you are on your way to becoming a master bowler!

THE BOWLING BALL TRACK

It is easy to determine the ball track, or roll of the ball. This is the worn band around its circumference that shows where the ball rolls down the lane. As it rolls, it picks up some of the lane dressing and the result is a clear band of wear around the ball.

If this band lies between your thumb hole and the finger holes, you are rolling what is called a full roller. It rolls over the entire circumference of the ball—really its equator—and it is an excellent mixing ball, although it does not hook much at the end of its travel. The bowler who rolls a full roller uses practically no wrist turn on the ball release.

The semiroller, also called a semispinner, is one that shows a track an inch or two outside the thumb hole. It is also called a three-quarter roller because that is about the amount of ball surface that is in contact with the lane. The bowler who rolls a semiroller has a good hook, and his or her release combines the squeeze or lift and slight wrist action as well.

The spinner ball is just what the term implies. Its track is way down on the ball and covers only a small part of the circumference of the ball. The ball spins down the lane much like a top. It does not have much mix or power. The spinner is rolled with a great deal of wrist turn at the point of ball release.

Your ball track can tell you how consistently you are delivering the ball. If the track is a narrow one, it shows consistency. If it varies several inches, it shows that you are not releasing the ball the same way every time.

Although it is interesting to consider the ball track and find out what kind of ball you roll, it is very difficult to change from one type of roll to another. There is something basic about the anatomy and musculature of every bowler that consigns each one to roll the ball in his or her own natural way. That way will turn out to be either a full roller or a semispinner most of the time. The important thing to remember is that you must try to deliver the ball every time with the same finger and wrist motion, whether it is with turn or without. Always make it the same and you are on your way to consistency in your delivery and to becoming a master bowler.

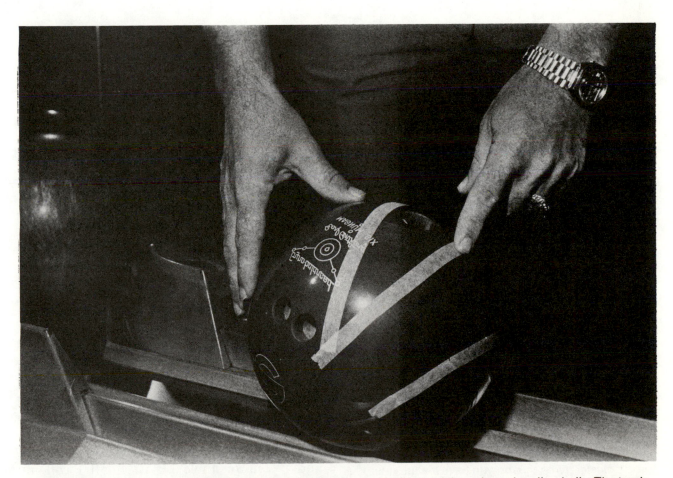

Here is a photo that shows the tracks of the full roller, the semiroller, and the spinner bowling balls. The track that rolls between the thumb hole and finger holes is the full roller. The bowler is pointing to the semiroller. The small track on the right side is the track of the spinner.

8
The Pins

THE TARGET PIN

In the heart of every spare you leave, there is one key pin that must be knocked down or else split conversion will fail. This pin is called the target pin and, in many cases, if you really concentrate on hitting only that

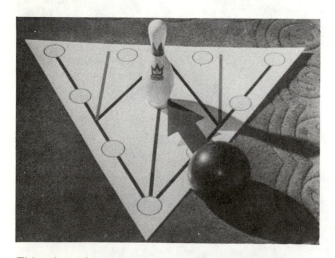

This photo is meant to illustrate the necessity to concentrate on the 5-pin, the so-called king pin of the pin cluster. Even though you have the full setup of ten pins in front of you on your first ball, try to imagine all of them gone, except for the hated 5-pin. Notice the angle you must use to knock it down.

pin, and ignore the rest of the pins that are standing, you will be successful.

Ordinarily, we are not talking about simple one- and two-pin spares when we talk about the target pin of a spare. We mean spares with three or more pins standing. One example is a 2–4–5–8 spare—the infamous "dinner bucket," one of the most dreaded spares of all for bowlers. First of all, the mere fact that these pins have been left shows that the bowler's first ball had less action than it should have had. That alone puts fear in the bowler's heart. Was it loss of action or was it just too much speed that carried the ball beyond the 5-pin? Was it incorrect angle? All of these thoughts cross the good bowler's mind as he or she confronts the 2–4–5–8 cluster.

"I have to get that 8-pin (the target pin in this case). Shall I move more to the right and try more angle on it? Shall I roll my normal ball from strike position, play it as a baby strike (with the 2–5 pocket acting as the usual 1–3) and get the 8-pin that way?"

These are some of the things that the bowler considers as he or she rolls at the 2–4–5–8 spare. Using the target pin concept, it is often possible for you to banish negative thoughts from your mind.

You see only the 8-pin in your mind's eye. The 2-, 4-, and 5-pins are not standing there at all. You envision the ball following its customary track with its normal action at the end and aim to hit the 8-pin solidly on its right side. In this case, the difficult four-pin cluster has become a simple one-pin spare you feel you can make "with your eyes closed."

Using the target pin thought will help you avoid worrying about many difficult multiple-pin spare leaves. You must constantly be aware of the target pin in the hard spares. The target pin thought will help you be very successful in converting many otherwise frightening leaves.

When your teammates congratulate you on making the "Polish Cathedral," for example, you can smile at them and say nonchalantly, "What Polish Cathedral? All I saw was the 9-pin!"

Del Warren and Dawson Taylor discuss the importance of the so-called king pin, the 5-pin. It is impossible for the ball to get all the pins by itself, so the bowler has to rely on the action of the pins, particularly the 5-pin, to help knock them all down. The 5-pin should be driven into the back row of pins to take out the 8-pin. Any other spinning help is a bonus. Remember the 5-pin; it is your hated enemy. You must get it out or lose a strike!

4-PIN AND 10-PIN TAPS

This photo illustrates the start of the 4-pin tap, which occurs on what appears to be a strike hit. The headpin is hit a little too high with the ball angling more to the right of the 5-pin than directly at it, as it should. The 2-pin is struck by the headpin on its right side and moves to its left rather than straight back to take out the 4-pin. The leave is a strike tap. Don't worry about getting it. You have had a good hit.

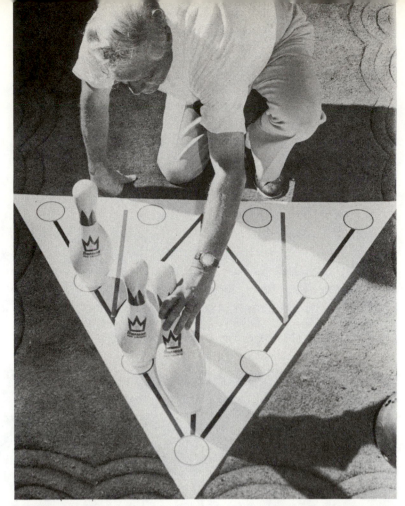

This photo shows how the 4-pin tap occurs. The first ball comes in high on the headpin, almost straight on, and drives the headpin into the 2-pin on the far right side of the 2-pin. The result is that the 2-pin, instead of moving back to take out the 4-pin as it normally would on a strike hit, moves to the left and wraps around the 4-pin, missing it. Don't worry about leaving 4-pins. You have rolled a strong ball a little too high on the headpin.

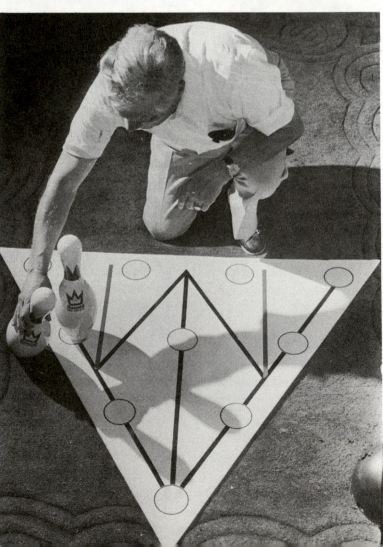

This photo illustrates the start of the so-called 10-pin tap. If the strike ball drives the 3-pin back so that it hits the 6-pin on its left side, the 6-pin responds by wrapping itself around the 10-pin and missing it. The answer usually is to get more angle into the 5-pin on the first ball so that the 2-pin is moved farther to the right. This tap happens to all bowlers. Don't worry about getting it. Sometimes it is just bad luck and the 10-pin will fall the next time on the same hit.

If the 6-pin goes off the pin deck sideways, it will often take the 10-pin with it. Sometimes it has to come off the sideboard to get it. Sometimes it remains in its vertical aspect and thus clears a smaller path than it usually does. That's when you get a 10-pin tap. The 6-pin is hit thinly on its left side and wraps around the 10.

9

The Spares

THE FOUR BASIC STARTING POSITIONS

If you study the illustration of the basic groups of spares, you will note that they are divided into four sections: right center group, left center group, far right group, and far left group. There is another varia-

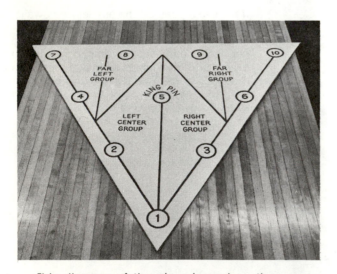

This diagram of the pins shows how they are broken down into various classifications of spares. Note that there are really only four groups that need to be memorized in order to organize all spare and split conversions.

tion, which is the left center group without the 5-pin standing. The same four positions would be true for the left-handed bowler except the variation would be the right center group without the 5-pin.

Basically, you can convert any one of these spare groups no matter which pin or pins in them are standing, if you observe the general rule of bowling across the lane at them. That means that for far right spares, you will bowl from the far left starting position. For a far left spare, you bowl from the far right starting position. For spares in the center groups, you don't move as far left or right, but bowl more from the center at them.

Most bowlers find their strike position with the left foot on the center dot of the approach. The right shoulder then comes into line with the strike line down the lane. The strike position is also useful for bowling what is called the "Brooklyn line" or "Brooklyn hit." The Brooklyn pocket is the 1–2 pocket for the right-hander (the reverse

(Left): This is the strike starting position. The left foot is placed at the center dot of the approach. The right shoulder is then in line with the strike line. *(Center):* This is the left center starting position. Usually it is five boards to the left of the normal strike position. This position is used to convert right center group spares. *(Right):* This is the far left starting position, twelve boards to the left of the normal starting position. It is used to convert far right spares and many splits that require the same angle.

for the left-hander). If the bowler rolls his or her normal strike ball one board to the left of the usual spot at the break of the boards (the spot on the lane where the diamond markers are inserted), the ball will cross over the headpin and carry a "Brooklyn hit," sparing the 1–2, the 1–2–4, the 1–2–4–8, as well as other combinations of the 1–2 leave.

It is very important that you learn these spare combinations by name. Learn to call them the instant you see them. "I've got a 2–4–5–8," for example. Incidentally, the pins are always named in numerical sequence. If you familiarize yourself with these spare- and split-making techniques, you will find that your bowling is more organized and will be more consistent.

The 2–4–7 Spare (Far Left Group)

Bowl this spare from the far right starting

This is the far right starting position. Your right foot moves to the right five boards (or more, depending upon the action of the bowler's ball). This position is used to convert far left spares and splits that require the same angle.

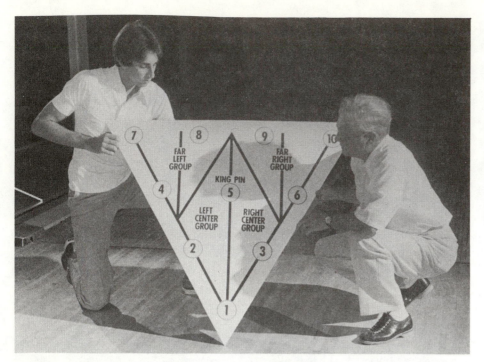

Del Warren and Dawson Taylor discuss the various pin groups for organized spare shooting. While there are basically four groups—the far left group, the far right group, the left center group, and the right center group—the presence or absence of the 5-pin in the left center group makes an additional variation for the conversion of that group.

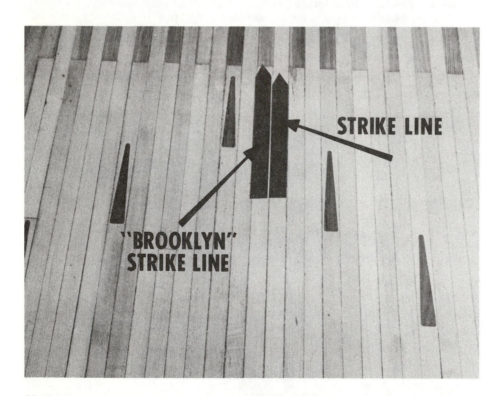

Notice the two black arrows that have been applied to the lane between the second and third "diamonds" from the right. The arrow on the right represents your normal "spot" board, or right, which takes your ball into the 1-3 "strike pocket." The arrow on the board to its left shows the line that the ball must travel to "cross over" the head pin and hit the 1-2 pocket for a "Brooklyn Hit." You do not change your starting position. You merely run one board left of your usual strike position line and the resulting "angle" does the work of bringing the ball into the 1-2 pocket.

position. Plan to hit the 2-pin on its left side and let the ball deflect into the 4-pin and possibly all the way to the 7-pin. If not, the 4-pin should take out the 7-pin. If you come in too high on the 4-pin, you may hit it too far on its right side and it will wrap around the 7-pin and miss it. This spare can also be made on the outside by hitting the 2-pin high on its right side and counting on pin

crucial that you have a strong enough first ball to avoid deflecting off the 2-pin and missing the 8-pin. This spare should be hit dead-on, flush on the right-hand side of the 2-pin so that the ball will carry through and take out the 8-pin. It is an exacting spare, too, because an inch too high or too low on the 2-pin, or a little less action than usual on the ball, leave the sleeper standing. You

THE 2–4–7 SPARE

THE 2–8 SPARE

deflection to take out the other two pins. Don't count on it. It is a risky shot. Always go for the pocket, here the 2–4 pocket, and by angling across the lane you should be able to let your ball carry through as well to get the 7-pin. Remember that when the ball hits the pin, rather than another pin, you are practically certain of converting the standing pin.

Master Bowling Practice. Practice making this spare both ways: on the outside by hitting the 2-pin on its right side, and then by hitting the 2–4 pocket. Practice picking the 10-pin off this cluster. Practice making an imaginary 4–7–10 split by hitting the 4-pin thinly on its left side and watching to see whether you would have forced it across the lane to get the 10-pin.

The 2–8 Spare

Bowl from the strike position, Brooklyn hit. The 8-pin is the sleeper in this leave and it is

should practice bowling the Brooklyn line strike position a great deal so that you are always prepared to make the 2–8, the 1–2–10, the 1–2–4, the 1–2–4–8 spares, where the ball must go through and get the 8-pin.

Master Bowling Practice. Practice bowling as if the 2-pin is not there at all. See only the 8-pin and plan to hit it on its right side. Let the 2-pin fall as if by accident. Practice picking the cherry on this spare by hitting the 2-pin in various places—high, low, and dead-on to note the action of the ball after it has contacted the 2-pin. Try to knock down the 8-pin without getting the 2-pin. This is a difficult shot and will require you to move to the right and go around the 2-pin. It is good practice for better control of the ball at all times.

The 1–2–4–7 Spare (Left Center Group)

Bowl from strike position, Brooklyn hit.

This spare is called the clothesline or the fence post. Whenever you leave more than one pin in a spare you are in danger of missing it. Here your danger is quadrupled. You must have the help of the 4-pin to take out the 7-pin after your ball has rolled into the Brooklyn 1–2 pocket. You must be certain, too, that your ball has action on it or you are sure to chop off one or more pins. If you move too far right in trying to make this spare, you may miss the headpin. Move

THE 1-2-4-7 SPARE

too far left and you may force the 4-pin around the 7-pin, leaving the 7-pin standing. It is possible to make this spare on the outside by hitting the headpin high on its right side and causing a chain reaction down the line. It works sometimes, but you cannot count on it.

Master Bowling Practice. Try to make this spare by alternating between the 1–2 pocket and hitting the headpin high on its right side. Then try to hit the headpin dead on and watch the action of the 4-pin as it fails to get the 7-pin. It will give you a better understanding of the way your strike ball sometimes fails in the same way. You can also practice getting the 2–7 left-hand baby split as well as the 2–4–7 spare. Another excellent idea is to practice picking the 7-pin off this cluster. It is very hard to do because your ball is coming in from the right and

usually catches the 4-pin before it gets to the 7-pin.

The 10-Pin Spare (Far Right Group)

Bowl from the far left starting position. Because this pin is in the last row of pins and because of the tendency of your ball to run left at the last moment of its track, you must roll your ball with greater speed than normal to cover it. Be sure that you square your body and your delivery toward the pin

THE 10-PIN SPARE

or toward the right-hand side of the 10-pin because you need as much room as you can get to convert it regularly. If you do not square your delivery, you are apt to pull it to the left and miss. Some bowlers imagine a pin standing in the channel to the left and aim for it, letting the ball take off at the last second to get the 10-pin. Always attempt to hit the 10-pin (or any other single-pin spare, for that matter) absolutely flush. Then, if there is any variance in the lane condition that might cause unusual final ball action, you will still manage to tick the pin and get it. If you are careless about making the 10-pin, not determined to hit it flush, you lessen your chances of making it and you will miss it.

Master Bowling Practice. Practice making the 10-pin on its right side, its left side, and then dead-on, absolutely flush. Practice on an imaginary 3–10 baby split by picturing the 3-pin still standing. Experiment by moving to the far right side of the lane and try to make the 10-pin by bowling directly down the right channel-edge boards. You will prove to yourself that the crosslane shot is the most successful one for you and for most bowlers.

The 1–2–8 Spare (Left Center Group)

This spare, the 1–2, the 1–2–4–8, the

THE 1–2–8 SPARE

1–2–4–7, and the wicked "washout" (the 1–2–10) are all bowled in exactly the same manner from the strike position, Brooklyn hit. Your spare ball must be rolled with action so as to ensure that it carries on through to get the 8-pin. A weak ball will result in "cherrying" the 8-pin, leaving it standing. You should make this spare every time. Sometimes bowlers have a tendency to move too far to the right and the result is that the ball deflects more off the 2-pin and misses the 8-pin on the left side. You cannot count on pin deflection to get the 8-pin if your ball fails to carry through and get it. Sometimes it helps to picture the 8-pin standing alone and ignore the 1–2 pair. Then, if you get the 8-pin with a strong ball you will, of course, get the 1–2 combination on the way to doing so.

Master Bowling Practice. When you prac-

tice on this spare, watch to see where you toss the 1-pin and see whether you would have converted the 10-pin if it had been left standing in a 1–2–10 washout. Try to pick the cherry; that is, leave the 8-pin by hitting the 1–2 combination high on the right side of the 2-pin. You may notice that your ball will still carry through to take the 8-pin. This happens only when there is strong action on the ball. A weak ball will be deflected away from the 8-pin.

THE 6–9–10 SPARE

The 6–9–10 Spare (Far Right Group)

Bowl from the far left starting position. Play this spare as a baby strike, remembering that the cluster is several feet farther away and that your ball will be running to the left at the end of its track. Try to hit this solidly in the 6–10 pocket, that is, neither too high nor too low on the 6-pin. It takes an exact hit not to cherry the 9-pin. Too high and the 6-pin goes to the right of the 9-pin; too low and it goes to the left of the 9-pin.

Master Bowling Practice. Try to leave the 9-pin intentionally by hitting the 6-pin so lightly on its right side that it goes to the left of the 9-pin. Then do the reverse. Hit the 6-pin head-on and try to force it to the right of the 9-pin. In this way you will obtain remarkable control of your spare ball. Try to chop the 10-pin off the cluster. It is difficult to do, but if you can do it, it is great practice for making the 6–7–10 split. You will learn how to hit the 6-pin very thinly in exactly the kind of action you need to throw it across the lane to take out an imaginary 7-pin.

The 1–2–10 Spare, the Washout

Bowl this spare from the strike position, Brooklyn hit, and you can make it every time. This spare usually results from a weak

THE 1–2–10 SPARE

ball that fails to reach the pocket and thus gets in behind the headpin. Your hit on the headpin must be high or you will cause it to wrap around the 10-pin, thus missing it. Be sure that your spare ball has action on it or it may flatten again and cause you to miss the spare.

Master Bowling Practice. Practice hitting the headpin in various ways—high left, center left, and weakly left—and note the action as it crosses the lane toward the 10-pin. Practice ignoring the presence of the 10-pin. Just roll your Brooklyn ball and let nature take its course. Practice hitting the 2-pin alone and letting it cross the lane to take out the 10-pin. It takes great accuracy to carry out these practice methods, but the results in greater control of the bowling ball are well worth any effort you put into the practice.

The 3–9 Spare

Bowl from the left center position. It is very easy to pick a cherry on this spare, so be careful that you do not move too far to the left. You want your ball to be coming in head-on on the 3-pin so that there is no deflection that might carry it to the right of the 9-pin. By hitting it head-on, you also have an extra chance that you can drive the 3-pin directly back to get the 9-pin, even if the ball does not carry through to get it

THE 3–9 SPARE

itself. Sometimes it helps to aim for the 9-pin as it it were standing alone. Draw your mental line through the 3-pin and shoot for the 9-pin, knowing that if you hit the 9-pin flush, you will take out the 3-pin on the way. This is a mean spare and requires a lot of concentration. You must roll a ball with action on this spare or you will get deflection to the right and miss the 9-pin.

Master Bowling Practice. Try to pick the cherry in practice. First get the 3-pin and let the 9-pin remain standing. Then try to get the 9-pin and leave the 3-pin standing. This is difficult to do and you may find that you will have to move far to the left to get the 9-pin regularly without at least ticking the 3-pin. Watch the deflection of your ball after it strikes the 3-pin. See whether it would have taken out a 6-pin if it had also been standing. By practicing on the 3-pin alone, you can practice on the 3–6–10 spare. You should be able to leave the 9-pin at will and the result will be that you will have great confidence on the 3–9 spare.

YOUR MOST DIFFICULT SPARE

Every bowler has a most difficult spare. For the right-handed bowler, it is often the 10-pin. For the left-hander, it is the counterpart of the 10-pin, the 7-pin. The reason that these two pins are so hard to convert is easy to understand if you examine the diagram of the placement of the pins on the pin deck. Notice that for every single-pin spare except the 7-pin and the 10-pin, the bowler has the advantage of the entire ball width on either side of the pin. That means that your single-pin target is the ball width plus the pin width plus the ball width again, or a total of twenty-three inches.

But the 7-pin and the 10-pin are only 2½ inches from the left-hand and right-hand channels, respectively. So your target area is reduced by seven inches, from twenty-three inches to sixteen inches. Add to the smaller target the realization that in most cases the bowler's ball is "working," that is, curving away from the target in its final hooking action, and you have another good reason why these single-pin spares are so difficult for most bowlers.

Be aware that the higher average bowler is apt to roll a ball with more hooking action than the lower average bowler. That fact, too, adds to the chances of the better bowler missing those one-pin spares.

The better bowler will also realize that since these two pins are in the last row, the ball must travel an additional two feet to reach the last line of pins. The lanes are not as well worn toward the corner pins. The result is more gripping action on the lane surface—more chance of the ball taking off in its curve, away from the 7-pin or the 10-pin.

I suggest that every good bowler turn a 10-pin or 7-pin nemesis into the spare he or she is most confident of converting successfully. The way to do this is to practice and practice and practice until it becomes second nature for you to approach them with the knowledge that you can make them every time. Once you have conquered these truly tough spares, you can then start to concentrate on your second- and third-toughest spares in order to add them to your confident spare list.

Let's talk about practicing the conversion of the 10-pin. I'd like to give you some ideas that I have used successfully—on the 10-pin, obviously, since I am right-handed. Early in my bowling career I realized that I would never achieve the excellence I was seeking unless I truly learned to put away that 10-pin every time without fail. Fortunately, I had a good friend, Larry Sisson, who managed Wy-Seven Lanes, the Detroit bowling establishment where I practiced most of the time.

Larry was sympathetic and cooperative. Although the lanes used automatic pinsetters, he would allow me to practice with the power off and the racks up. I had another young friend who acted as pin boy in the old-fashioned manner, setting pins the way they used to be set in the old days by putting them up by hand in the pit. My pin-setting friend would get into the pit at the end of the lane and put up that 10-pin every time I knocked it down. At first, we had an agreement that if I missed it one time in twenty I owed him a beer. When we were first practicing that way, I think I bought him a case of beer a week. But gradually I began to make that 10-pin time after time, sometimes as many as fifty, even sixty, times in a row.

I would ask Larry to slick up the lanes I was using for practice, that is, to polish them to a high gloss so that the ball wouldn't take as much at the end of its travel. When I did that, I could shoot straighter at the pin and my ball would not dive to the left and miss the 10-pin at the end. Another time I asked Larry to fix his practice lane so that it ran as much as it could. He would not polish the lane as much and would do some other tricks with the lane-surfacing materials. The result was exactly what I wanted, a true running lane, the hardest possible condition for making the 10-pin. I continued to practice making the spare. I had to move farther to my left than I did when the lane was stiff. I also learned that I had to speed up my ball considerably to delay the final hook of the ball to the left. I practiced killing the ball by altering my hand position and giving the ball less lift as I released it. I found that under extreme running conditions I made the 10-pin most of the time when I used both corrections—added speed and the ball-killing action.

At last I was learning how to adapt my bowling style to the lane conditions. I recommend that you follow the same procedure I used. If you cannot find an unused lane for individual pin setting, then settle for using the entire rack. Roll your first ball of the frame at the 10-pin. Score yourself with a strike symbol if you have converted it. Then, on your second ball, work on converting the pins that are left standing. You will have some interesting combinations. I'll bet you even have a "Polish Cathedral" (the 1–5–6–8–9–10) once in a while. In conclusion, my advice is to win the battle of the 7-pin and the 10-pin the way I did. Practice, practice, practice!

The 7-pin and the 10-pin are only 2½ inches from the channel. Your target area is 7 inches smaller than it would be for an 8-pin or a 9-pin. That's why it is so easy to miss a 10-pin!

10
The Splits

THE FIT-IT-IN-BETWEEN SPLITS

As you can see in the illustration above, you have about two more inches in ball width than the distance between the two pins, the 5–6. There are several other similar leaves that occur with regularity—the 4–5, the 7–8, and the 9–10. Along with the two so-called baby splits—the 3–10 and the 2–7—they are all classified as fit-it-in-between splits, meaning that you should be able to convert any one or all of them by rolling your ball between them and taking them both out at one time. Remember your angles and try to make them exactly in the middle. There is a little room to spare for deflection of the ball one way or the other, but you should not count on it. The master bowler should make all the fit-it-in-between spares every time.

The 2-7 Fit-it-in-between Split
(Left-hand Baby Split)

Bowl from the far right starting position. You can aim for the left side of the 2-pin and let the ball deflect into the 7-pin, or you

FIT-IN-BETWEEN SPLIT

47

may find it useful to imagine that you are aiming for the ghost pin (the 4-pin), planning to hit it high on its right side, and then take out the 7-pin with the ball or with the pin. This split is easier for the right-handed bowler than its counterpart, the 3–10, because the bowler's ball is curving into the last pin; in the 3–10, it is curving away from it. Practice this split a great deal. You should convert it every time.

THE 2-7 SPLIT

Master Bowling Practice. Try making this split on the outside, that is, by hitting the 2-pin on its right side so as to deflect it into the 7-pin. Prove to yourself that the best way to make it is not on the outside because that shot is more difficult. It is always better to take as many pins as you possibly can with the ball rather than rely on pin deflection. Remember that pins can fly straight through as well as sideways. When they go straight through, they are sometimes ineffective in hitting other pins in the rows behind them. Practice making an imaginary 2–7–10 split by hitting the 2-pin on its left side and watching to see whether or not it would have taken out an imaginary 10-pin.

The 3–10 Fit-it-in-between Split (Right-hand Baby Split)

Bowl from the far left position. There are several different methods of making this split. You should be aware of all of them and then, through practice, find the method that suits your mind and game best and stick with it. Do not change it or vary it. The first way is to plan to make the fit by hitting the 3-pin on its right side, letting the ball deflect to take the 10-pin. The second way is to shoot for a head-on hit of an imaginary 6-pin (the pin that is missing in

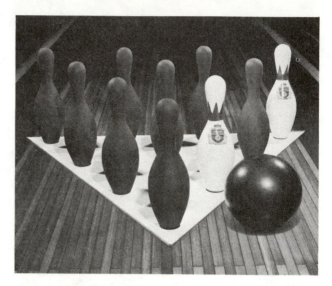

THE 3-10 SPLIT

the setup) and let the other two pins fall as if by accident. A third method is to aim at only the 10-pin, planning to let the ball move to the left at the last moment to take out the 6-pin. A fourth method involves finding your particular spot at the break of the boards, somewhere near the third to fourth board, and rolling from far left over that spot with your normal board. Some bowlers kill the ball on this split, which really should be a consistently converted spare for the master bowler. They do this by greatly increasing its speed and also by not imparting finger lift as the ball is released. This is a dangerous practice, because you have been training yourself to lift the ball in the same way on every delivery. Once you start varying your lift, you may find it difficult to regain consistency on your first ball. Some bowlers can do it, that is, kill the ball successfully and yet get back to their normal lift immediately thereafter. Some bowlers cannot do it. You will have to experiment and find your own best method.

Master Bowling Practice. Practice making this split on the outside, that is, by hitting the 3-pin on its left side so as to deflect it over to the 10-pin. It might be a handy shot some day when the lanes are running too much to hold the ball on line at the last moment. Practice making the 10-pin only, then the 3-pin only. You will increase your general accuracy with this practice as it takes a perfect flush hit on either pin to accomplish this trick.

The 4–5 Fit-it-in-between Split

Start in strike position, Brooklyn hit, and you will be able to fit your ball between these two pins. This split is usually missed on the left because the bowler forgets that the pins are farther away in the third row, twenty-two inches beyond the headpin. Sometimes it is wise to overcorrect to the right, and you may increase your chances of fitting this split. Another trick in making it is to imagine that you have only the missing 8-pin, and to shoot for it. If you make the 8-pin flush, you will fit the front two pins. This idea may work, too, because you may

be more relaxed shooting for a one-pin imaginary spare rather than a split.

Master Bowling Practice. Try to make the 5-pin alone and then the 4-pin alone. Then try to fit your ball in the middle and make both pins. Try bowling from strike position to see where your ball comes in on the 5-pin. Then make the correction to the Brooklyn strike line and watch your ball make the fit, proving that the Brooklyn line does work on this split.

The 5–6 Fit-it-in-between Split

This is an awkward split because you rarely encounter it and because you bowl for it from a starting position that you use less frequently than the others. This split is missed most often on the left, that is, by knocking down the 5-pin and missing the 6-pin. The reason for this is that you are using a line not as heavily traveled as usual. The consequence is a tendency for the ball to work more than normal at the end. Be sure to allow for more correction to the right of the line than your eye tells you to take, since the pins are in the third row and your ball may take off to the left on its curve in the last foot of its travel. If you leave this split often, it is a sign of inaccuracy on the first ball, crossing over with the ball working

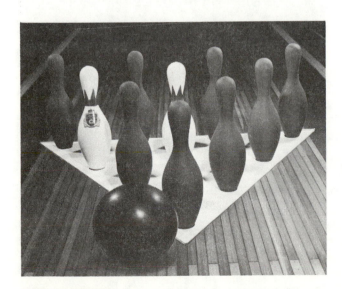

THE 4–5 SPLIT

THE 5–6 SPLIT

away from the 5-pin. It indicates that you should change your angle of attack so as to get into the 1–3 pocket.

Master Bowling Practice. Try to make this split from your normal strike starting position. It will be more difficult than from the left center position but should give you an idea of strike ball control. Practice hitting the 5-pin thinly so as to deflect it to take out an imaginary 7-pin. Watch to see where the 5-pin leaves the pin deck, over the 7-pin spot, the 8-pin spot, or straight back, and you can tell how thin your hit was on the 5-pin. Practice making the 5-pin alone, hitting it absolutely flush, then the 6-pin alone, again absolutely flush. Then work on the fit. You will develop amazing control if you practice this sweep from one pin to the other and back again. You should make the 5–6 split every time—that is, if you are a master bowler!

THE SLIDE-IT-OVER SPLITS

As you can see from this illustration and from examining the photographs of the slide-it-over splits that follow, it is evident that if one of the pins in the split is in the row in front of one or more of the other pins—even if the split is wide open, like the 6–7–10—it is entirely possible for you to convert the split into a spare. You do so by managing to strike the pin in the front thinly, by merely touching it with your ball and forcing it to fly across the lane at an oblique angle and take out the remaining pin or pins. For the right-handed bowler it is easier to make a slide-it-over split when the ball action required is one that brings the ball in on the right-hand side of the 6-pin or the 5-pin because the natural curve of the ball from right to left helps the bowler make the conversion. Splits that require the pins to be moved across the lane from left to right are harder for the right-handed bowler. The reverse, of course, is true for the left-handed bowler. These splits are well

worth making, especially if the result of a game depends on a final pin count of only a few pins. When count is not important, try for the split; if you miss it, you lose only a pin or two. If count is important, always get as many pins as you can.

The 5–7 Slide-it-over Split

You will convert this split regularly if you bowl for it from the Brooklyn hit strike position. That is, bowl with your target at the break of the boards, one board to the left of your usual strike position pocket-hit line. It may also be necessary for you to move your starting position one board left if the first line suggested does not work for you. Remember that your ball is traveling twenty-two inches beyond the headpin spot before it contacts the 5-pin. It has more distance to travel on the lane, more friction with its surface, and thus has a stronger tendency to take off to the left and miss the 5-pin. Experiment with this split until you find the best solution for you. Remember that you cannot expect nearly as high a conversion average on the 5–10 split as you might have on the 5–7 split. This is because, in the case of the 5–10, your ball is moving away from the crucial 5-pin; in the other situation, it is going toward the 5-pin, helping it make the conversion. If you leave

THE 5–7 SPLIT

many of these 5–10 splits, it is a sure sign that your ball is losing action at the pocket. It is also a sign that you are rolling the ball with too much speed.

Master Bowling Practice. Practice aiming at an imaginary 8-pin, forgetting about the two pins that are standing. Pretend they aren't there at all. Practice moving to the far right starting position to see whether your chances of conversion of the split improve.

Practice moving far left to see if your chances improve.

Practice hitting the 5-pin lightly on its right side, then head-on, and then lightly on its left side.

Practice hitting the 10-pin lightly on its right side, then flush, and then on its left side.

The 5-10 Slide-it-over Split

Bowl from strike position, or Brooklyn hit. Much like the 8–10, this split is a sure indicator of a weak first ball, one that has flattened and died in the pocket. If you frequently leave this split or the 8–10, you are not putting enough finger action on the ball, nor enough finish at the end of the ball track. You may be using an improper angle—one that is coming in too high on the headpin and not enough into the 1–3 pocket—to get the 5-pin out of the setup. If

you find that you have difficulty making this split using the Brooklyn line, you might try moving a little to the left at your start, maintaining the Brooklyn line at the break of the boards. Or you may find that you have the most success with this split by moving both start and line a board or so to the left. You will have to experiment and find your best line and angle. Once you find it, don't change it. Use it every time and you will gain great consistency in making this split.

Master Bowling Practice. Practice making the 5-pin on its right side, then flush, and then on its left side. Note how high on the 5-pin you must strike it in order to produce the proper trajectory for it to cross the lane and take out the 10-pin. Practice cutting the 5-pin so thinly on its left side that you force it across and in front of the 10-pin.

The 4-7-9 Slide-it-over Split

Bowl from the far right starting position. Ignore the 4-pin and the 9-pin. Aim for the 7-pin alone and try to hit it less than directly, more toward its left side. In that way you will shave the 4-pin on its left side and force it to the right where it can take out the 9-pin. You should convert this split frequently because the 9-pin is a foot closer to

THE 5-10 SPLIT

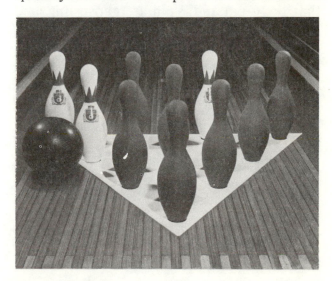

THE 4-7-9 SPLIT

the 4-pin than the 10-pin would be if you were shooting for the 4–7–10 split. Furthermore, it takes less power to send it as far as the 9-pin than it does to send it clear across the lane. If you frequently leave this split, it is an indication that you are coming in too high on the headpin and that you should adjust your angle more toward the 3-pin.

Master Bowling Practice. Practice making the 4–7 spare on the outside, that is, by hitting the 4-pin on its right side.

Pretend the 9-pin is not standing at all and you are making the 4–7 by a thin conversion—a light hit on the left side of the 4-pin.

Practice hitting the 4-pin so thinly on its right side that you wrap it around the 7-pin and thus miss the 7-pin.

Practice on the 9-pin alone, hitting it flush on its right side, and then on its left side.

Practice hitting the 9-pin so thinly on its right side that you drive it across the lane toward the 7-pin. See whether you can convert the 7–9 split this way.

The 6–7–10 Slide-it-over Split

Start from the far left position and shoot to hit the 10-pin lightly on its right side, not fully or head on. Sometimes it helps to imagine that only the 10-pin is standing, that the 6-pin and 7-pin are ghost pins, and

that you are shooting for the 10-pin only. Hitting the 10-pin lightly will cause your ball to come in strongly at the last second on the right side of the 6-pin. If you hit it just right, it will be clipped over the lane to take out the 7-pin. Be sure not to ease up on this conversion. In fact, it is often necessary to speed up your ball in order to lessen the action at the end of its travel and keep it on the right side of the 6-pin. Besides, a slow ball may impart so little force to the 6-pin that even if it slides it across the lane it may not have enough power to take the 7-pin out. That is most discouraging after an accurate shot has been made in the first place.

Master Bowling Practice. Try to take out the 10-pin without touching the 6-pin.

Try to make an intentional chop of the 6-pin off the 10-pin.

Try hitting the 6-pin on its left side so that it takes out the 10-pin.

Try hitting the 6-pin so lightly on its left side that it wraps around and misses the 10-pin.

The 4–7–10 Slide-it-over Split

Bowl this split from the far right starting position. Plan to tick the 4-pin on its left side so as to slide it over across the lane and take out the 10-pin. The 4-pin must be hit extremely thinly or it will angle more to-

THE 6-7-10 SPLIT

THE 4-7-10 SPLIT

ward the 9-pin spot and thus fail to make the conversion. It sometimes helps to pretend that the 4-pin and the 10-pin are not there at all and that you are merely converting a simple 7-pin spare by hitting it less than fully. In your league or tournament bowling it is important always to remember the importance of the count of two pins rather than one, especially if you are working on a strike. Unless it is extremely important for the result of a game that you make the split, always get the two pins rather than lose count.

Master Bowling Practice. Practice hitting the 7-pin alone and leaving the 4-pin and 10-pin standing.

Practice hitting the 4-pin high on its right side, flush, and then lightly on its left side. Note where you must strike the 4-pin so as to have it take out the 9-pin or the 10-pin.

Practice on the 10-pin. See if you can get it with a ball falling off into the channel on the right. Hit the 10-pin flush.

Pretend that the 6-pin is standing and make the imaginary 6–10 pin spare.

The 4–6–7–10 Impossible Split

This split, also called double pinochle, is a bowler's horror not only because it is impossible to convert but because it is a sure sign that the bowler has rolled a weak first ball. Be conscious of your count and make certain you convert at least two of these pins. If you are bowling in competition, bowl for the two easiest pins and make sure you get them. Don't experiment or try to be a hero in your bowling league by aiming for the 4–6–10 or the 6–7–10 cluster out of this split. You will invariably miss an extra pin, or you could miss all of them and lose count.

Master Bowling Practice. There are innumerable practice opportunities when you encounter this split in practice.

Practice making the 4–7–10 split by hitting the 4-pin lightly on its left side.

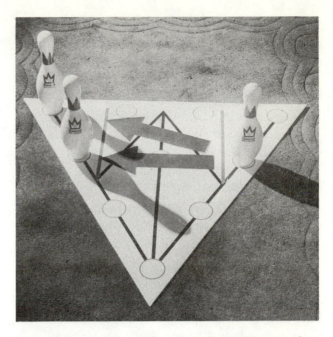

This photo of the 4–6–7 setup shows how much more difficult an angle there is for the 6-pin to convert the 4-pin. On the other hand, you can see that the angle toward the 7-pin is much more favorable. There is more chance for the 6-pin to slide over and get it. That is why open splits on the same lane are called impossible splits. They are made very rarely, however. It takes great skill to shave the 6-pin so closely that it moves straight across the lane to get the 4-pin.

Imagine the 9-pin standing and see whether you can make the 4–7–9 split.

Practice making the 6–7–10 split by hitting the 6-pin lightly on its right side.

Try to get the 7-pin alone and then the 10-pin alone.

THE 4-6-7-10 IMPOSSIBLE SPLITS

Try to leave the 7-pin by hitting the 6-pin lightly on its right side and then do the same thing on the other side.

Hit the 6-pin lightly on its left side and leave the 10-pin.

By practicing like this you will gain great control of your ball and will not fear any spare or split.

The 8–10 Impossible Split

This split and its counterpart, the 5–10, usually occur when the ball dies or flattens on a pocket 1–3 hit. It is a certain sign that the first ball was weak. One answer is always to get more action on the first ball; another is to correct the angle so that the ball comes into the 1–3 pocket more from the right side, allowing you to take the 5-pin and thus the 8-pin as well. If you are bowling in competition, be sure that you get one or the other of these two pins to increase your count. This split is made so rarely that it is practically useless to try converting it.

The 8–10 Impossible Split

Master Bowling Practice. Practice getting the 8-pin by bowling from the Brooklyn hit strike position.

Then try bowling from your normal strike position, at the strike line, and watch what happens at the end of the ball's travel. You should be able to skin the 8-pin on its right side, just barely making it.

Then practice making the 10-pin, first flush or head-on, then on its right side, and then on its left side.

The 4–6 Impossible Split

This split, like double pinochle (the 4–6–7–10), happens when your ball hits too high on the headpin. It is obvious that you have crossed too far to the left on your first ball and must get back into the 1–3 pocket. Consider changing your line to the right or rolling your ball a little faster. If you are bowling in competition, be careful to count the one pin for your score. Since it is rarely made, don't be a hero and try to convert it, missing both pins and losing count.

The 4–6 Impossible Split

Master Bowling Practice. Practice converting your most difficult pin of these two. If you are troubled by spares on the left side, work on the 4-pin. If your problem is on the right side, practice making the 6-pin.

You can also try imagining that the 4–7–10 is standing and that you are trying to convert that split. Watch to see how your ball reacts and whether or not you would have made it.

In the same way you can picture a 6–7–10 split; by clipping the 6-pin very thinly on its right side, you can tell whether you would have converted the 6–7–10.

Make good use of every split you get. Practice, practice, practice!

The 7–9 Impossible Split

Be aware of count and always make certain that you convert at least one of these pins. If you are bowling in practice and leave this split, always practice on your most difficult pin. If you have been missing the 7-pin, practice on it. If the 9-pin has been giving you trouble, work on it. Try moving one board to the left or right from your normal far right starting position and watch what effect the move has on your ball action. You may do the same thing working on the 9-pin, bowling from the left center position. In league play, of course, do not experiment; rather, get your easiest pin to assure yourself of the pin count.

Master Bowling Practice. Try to make this split in practice. Move to the far left and try to catch the 9-pin so lightly on its right side that you slide it over to take out the 7-pin. It is almost impossible, but it can be made once in a very long while. While practicing hitting the 9-pin very thinly, vary your practice to hit it fully, and then lightly

The 7–9 Impossible Split

on its left side. Do the same thing with the 7-pin, hitting it first on its right side, then flush, and then lightly on its left side. Notice the pin action in hitting the 7-pin lightly. Your ball will move away farther to the left, and it is truly impossible to make the 9-pin with the 7-pin sliding over to take it out. The ball angle increases your chances of making it from the other side, so if you ever must make the split to win a game, the only way to try it is from the 9-pin side.

11
Practice

AT THE LANES

Practice intelligently every time you do practice. Don't ever bowl for fun if you are seriously considering becoming a champion bowler. In my opinion, bowling for fun means rolling the ball at random targets without concentrating on what you are doing with your target line, your footwork, or your timing. If you get into the habit of bowling for fun with other people who distract you from your primary purpose, you will halt any progress you may have made toward bowling perfection and may even take steps backward, losing the talent you have already developed.

I do not maintain that you should never bowl merely for recreation, but I do insist that when you bowl in circumstances that do not demand your best scores you should not lose sight of your eventual desire for perfection. You must concentrate on every bowling shot you make and even use the distractions that are present—such as bad form exhibited by other bowlers, or ex-

traneous noise—as a testing ground to help you improve your ability to concentrate under difficult circumstances.

When you practice, do not practice haphazardly. Always have one or more goals in mind as the main object of a particular practice session. Let me suggest a few thoughts to you on practice methods that have worked for many good bowlers who have mastered the game over the years.

The most important thing about every practice session is that you make sure you are rolling the ball properly. Therefore, the first few deliveries you make in a practice session should always be done with a view to observing the efficacy of your timing and the consistency of your delivery. Are you delivering the ball out over the line so that you achieve your customary good roll on the ball? In other words, if you usually put the ball down from twelve to fourteen inches out over the foul line with what is called moderate loft, you should be sure you

Here is an illustration of the use of sheets of white paper taped onto the lane to show where your ball is hitting the lane in your delivery. You can check your consistency in direction as well as in amount of loft out onto the lane by the way the marks show up on the paper. You should practice until your cluster of marks is consistently in the same place within a fraction of an inch or two every time you roll the ball.

are placing the ball at that distance, not short of it or beyond it. Once you have assured yourself that you are in normal form, you can start to work on the goal of that particular practice session.

Let us say that you have been having trouble converting the 5–7 split. With the advent of automatic pin setters with full ten-pin settings, it seems that it might be difficult to practice making just the 5–7 split. This is not so. Here's how to do it. On the first ball of your practice frame, merely move to the left and practice making the right-hand baby split, the 3–10. You will find that more often than not the 5-pin and 7-pin will still be standing after your first ball has taken out the 6- and 10-pins. You will also have a few other pins left as well, but ignore them. You are working on the 5–7 split only. Then, on your second ball of the frame, you have a practice shot at the split.

Whether or not you can use this practice method will depend to a great extent on the type of ball you roll. It may be necessary for the strong bowler to work first on the 6- and 10-pins only, in order to make sure to leave the 5-pin for the second ball. My point is that you should experiment. Find out what works for you and what does not work. Find exactly how far you need to move to the left of your usual starting position in order to cause your ball to come in lightly on the 5-pin and snap it over to the 7-pin every time. It may be a board to the left, or two boards left of your usual starting position. It may even be necessary to move your target spot at the darts one board to the right of your usual spot.

As you practice making the 5–7 split, keep an accurate count of the number of times you convert it. Eventually you should build your odds of making the 5–7 split conversion to at least 50 percent. I have known good bowlers who will get even money that they can convert the 5–7. And they will take your money from you because they do convert it more than half the time!

Another excellent idea is to use a stopwatch to time your bowling delivery. Ask a friend to help you do this. You should also have a notebook in which to record your performance. I suggest that you time ten different successive bowling deliveries and then compare the times for each. Several segments should be timed separately. First, have yourself timed from the moment you leave the banquette of seats to get your ball from the ball-return rack to the moment you take your starting position at the line. That interval is the first to examine for consistency.

Then time yourself from the instant of your first move toward the line up to the explosion point as you deliver the ball out over the line. You may be one of those fortunate individuals for whom the first moves by hand and foot occur at the same time, or you may be one of those who starts with the hand or the foot first. It does not

matter. Start the clock with that first move toward the line, whatever it is.

You should get a third set of figures, as well: the time it takes for your ball to travel down the lane to the pocket. You will find that time interval useful in speeding up or slowing down your ball at a later time.

At first you will find that there are inconsistencies in these various time intervals. But once you recognize them, you should be able to start to standardize the intervals until they become as automatically consistent as your breathing. Don't hurry, but don't make yourself overly self-conscious about it. Set your own pace, and once you have found it, don't vary it. You may find it useful to count to yourself "one thousand and one, one thousand and two, one thousand and three" and so on, as you establish the rhythm you want in your bowling delivery when you take your ball from the rack and assume your starting position. If you carry out this practice regularly, you will find that the counting becomes unnecessary since you have established your routine and set it once and for all in your own determined rhythm.

It is very interesting to use a stopwatch in observing the present stars of the bowling world. You can frequently see them on national television, and if you time one bowler a number of times in successive frames you will notice great consistency in all respects of the pro's game, from the time to get set at the line to the time elapsed between the first move and the delivery at the line. You will also note variances of several seconds from bowler to bowler. It might be wise to imitate a bowler whose style and tempo seem to fit your own. In the long run, of course, you will work out your own individual timing and general style.

I recommend that you find one particular bowling lane in your vicinity and turn it into your regular practice arena. It need not be the one at which you regularly bowl your league games. However, it could be, provided it meets a number of other qualifications I would like to submit for consideration before you choose your practice lane.

First of all, you need an atmosphere that is as quiet as possible. Therefore, find a lane and a time (or times) when you can be absolutely alone on the lanes. This may take some doing—even some rearrangement of your own schedule to fit the "dead" time at the lanes.

Make the lane operator your friend and confidant. In many cases lane operators, especially countermen, are good bowlers and often good observers of bowlers. Tell the operator that your goal is to improve and that you would appreciate any help he or she can offer. This individual can do many things for you, such as seeing to it that you bowl against good bowling pins, that the lanes are surfaced well for you, and that you are left alone to practice. When other practice bowlers come in to roll a game or two, the operator can put them on lanes far away from you in order to insulate you from distracting noise and confusion.

I have used several practice methods successfully in my bowling career and I would like to recommend that you try one or all of them. They helped me raise my average from the low 160s to the 200 range within three years.

The first concerns perfecting a straight-line approach to the foul line. Just as you put down a practice guideline in your own recreation room, a friendly lane operator may permit you to do the same thing in practice on one of the lanes. Use a "Scotch" type of opaque masking tape and put it down so that your approach straddles it. Use the masking tape as a guideline for several of your bowling lines. Set it up for a normal second-arrow straightaway shot and check to see that your feet do not cross the line. Using such a line will help you concentrate on squareness at the line because later,

when you bowl without the masking tape, your mind's eye will still see it on the lane and remind you to use the proper footwork. You can set the masking tape delivery line so that you can work on an inside angle delivery, on a channel shot on the far right side, or on any angle you want to perfect.

The second trick I recommend involves the use of two large sheets of paper with carbon paper between the sheets. You will need the lane operator's consent for this practice, but he will probably give it to you. Tape the sheets down beyond the foul line on the right-hand side where you normally deliver your strike ball. You will plan to make ten successive deliveries, all supposedly strike balls, that is, as if you were bowling the same ball to the pocket every time. After you have made the ten deliveries, you will take up the sheets of paper and the carbon marks of the impact spots where the ball was set down on the lane will give you a great deal of information about the consistency or inconsistency of your delivery. If you see that you are varying by an inch or two to the right or left of your intended spot, you must work to make your footwork more repetitive, more exact. If the carbon marks show that you are lofting the ball out a few inches over the line in one delivery, and then a foot or more on another, it is an indication that you must perfect your footwork and timing so that you reach the same proximity to the foul line each time you roll the ball. These carbon sheets can be prepared in sets and should be numbered and dated. If you use them frequently, you are bound to see an improvement in your bowling.

When you practice on any particular spare or split, be sure that you keep an accurate count of how many times you make the spare or split. I have found an excellent method of practice to work on the 3–10 right-hand baby split with my first ball of a practice frame. I aim for the 6-pin one time, for the right side of the 3-pin another time, and then try to chop the 10-pin off all alone. Then, on my second ball, I have any number of possibilities for spare practice. I can practice on the 1-3 pocket, the 1-2 pocket, or even move far right and work on far left spaces.

Practice intelligently and you are bound to improve. I am sure that you can and will develop practice techniques far more interesting and productive than mine. Good luck!

AWAY FROM THE LANES

Here are some good tips on how to practice bowling at your leisure in your home or office. The first requisite is a vinyl-tile floor that you can polish to an approximation of the conditions you find on the bowling lane. Some dance wax will usually do the trick. Then take some tape—adhesive or masking tape—and lay out a mock approach for yourself. Set up the foul line and a T-bar, the line on which you intend to practice. Then walk the line many times a day, keeping your eye on an imaginary target out over your mock foul line.

The idea is to instill in your mind the path you want to take on every delivery of the bowling ball. You can practice your first step, the distance, and the direction by putting a mark on the tape where you want your first step to be. Then take your ball and, again watching your spot out over the line, make your first step and the coinciding pushaway of the ball. Then look down to see that your step has gone precisely the distance you want.

A metronome is another excellent aid in perfecting your timing. The bowling delivery should be as smooth and rhythmic as a dance step. With ingenuity in practice you can achieve this goal and become a master bowler.

Here's the way to practice making your first step of the bowling delivery in exactly the same way every time. With the mock lane in front of you, mark the taped line at the precise spot you want your first step to end. Then, assuming a bowling position start and keeping your eye on an imaginary target down the line, step out without looking at your foot. Then note how close you have come to repeating the step every time. Your first step is the most important. Work on it!

Dawson Taylor illustrates the use of the mock lane in your own recreation room. It is most important that you practice your pushaway to make certain that it coincides with your first step. By walking the taped line hundreds of times you will impress upon your mind a target line that you will see when you bowl on the actual lane. It is an amazing phenomenon, but it works!

Dawson Taylor shows how to use the mock lane to standardize your delivery, particularly your first step. Holding the ball in front of you in your normal starting position, move it out at the same instant that you take your first step. Then check to make sure your step is made in exactly the same place each time—no farther, no shorter, and directly on line.

This is an exercise designed to impress on your mind the necessity of a free-flowing backswing and forward swing. Assume a mock starting position at your imaginary bowling lane. Keep your eye on a particular spot out on the lane as you swing your bowling arm back and forth in a bowling arc. Try to do this 100 times a day. It will help groove your swing.

Here is an exercise to help you increase the freedom and mobility of your backswing. It also helps to impress on your mind the necessity for leaning forward as you deliver the ball. You can practice this exercise, too, as a way of visualizing in your mind where your thumb is during your backswing. Good bowlers always know exactly what their hand position and finger position are at any part of the bowling delivery.

12
Faults

Here are some illustrations of the most common faults in bowling. Most of them are caused by erratic footwork. If the bowler does not approach the line in a straight walk, his or her arm is apt to leave the side of the body, moving to the outside and causing the fault known as *side-wheeling*. The reverse action, with the ball coming around behind the body, causes the fault known as *topping the ball*.

It is most important that all bowlers obtain professional instruction so that they can understand their own faults and correct them.

Del Warren shows us the fault called side-wheeling. The bowler brings the ball around behind him, turning his body away from the pins and away from his target line. This is a serious fault that can be corrected by making sure that you remain square to the line throughout your delivery.

(Top left): This is another demonstration of the fault called side-wheeling. It happens when the bowler lets the ball get away from his side in the backswing. The bowler's elbow is bent rather than straight, adding to the ill effect of the fault. Be sure to keep your arm close to your body, your elbow unbroken, your shoulder high (not dropped), and you can get rid of the fault of side-wheeling. *(Top right):* Del Warren demonstrates the fault known as the dropped shoulder. From this bodily position it is difficult, if not impossible, to get proper action on the ball. It usually happens when the bowler slants in toward the pins on the delivery and then realizes that he has done so and tries to correct it at the last moment.

Del Warren demonstrates the fault of rushing the line. This is a common fault among all bowlers, great ones as well as average ones. The result of rushing the line is that the ball cannot be delivered at the proper point in its descending arc and thus comes off the bowler's fingers without action. The symptom of this fault is the sliding foot turned away from the line. Watch to make sure your sliding foot is headed straight for your target line.

13
The Unorthodox Bowler

In every sport, there are stars who excel in spite of their departure from the accepted, or normal, techniques, whether they are striking a baseball or rolling a bowling ball. Stan Musial, one of the greatest hitters in baseball history, was known for his strange crouch and the way he sprang at the ball. Lou Campi, one of the finest bowlers of all time, was called "Wrong Foot Louie" because he ended up at the foul line with the "wrong" foot—the right—sliding ahead. In spite of what appeared to be an awkward, unbalanced delivery, Campi got the job done. In the early days of televised bowling, he met the best bowlers head to head and defeated every one of them. The television series ended before anyone conquered him!

In my earlier book, *The Secret of Bowling Strikes,* I reported knowing a champion high-average bowler who always converted the 10-pin spare by bowling straight down the last two or three boards on the right side of the lane, rather than rolling across the lane from the far left side in the usual way.

He never missed, either, as far as I remember.

Today we see a number of unorthodox bowlers entering the championship bowling scene, and they are thriving in spite of their unorthodox deliveries. One bowler who comes to mind is young Wayne Webb, who dangles the ball at his side, moving it back and forth slightly until the rhythm strikes him as right. Then he takes a couple of steps forward, stops suddenly, and makes another surge of steps to the line. There he delivers a powerful ball that travels down the far right-hand side of the lane until it makes a tremendous move toward the left and into the pocket.

Webb gets the pins moving to the left off the sideboards and achieves tremendously successful action. Unorthodox, yes, but also successful.

Something else we are seeing today is the rise of the power bowler. This is the bowler who is so physically strong that he appears capable of throwing the ball overhand down the lanes and knocking down all the pins. Mark Roth, 1979 Bowler of the Year, comes to mind as a typical power bowler. Mark even varies the number of steps he takes to the line. He takes a few stutter steps and then cranks the ball far behind him and upward. His hand and wrist open in clockwise fashion, violating all the usual rules of good bowling technique. But when Mark delivers his ball out on the lane, the result is one of the most explosively destructive balls in bowling history. His ball moves so sharply to the left at the far end of his ball track that it is sometimes necessary for him to loft it out onto the lanes almost as far as the break of the boards—the darts that are fifteen feet down the lane.

Mark is extremely successful, and has won more than $100,000 a year for several years on the professional bowling tour. He is a unique bowler. His hand gets tremendous wear as he spins his ball off the thumb and lofts it so far out on the lane. There is certainly some question about how long his fingers and body will be able to take the terrible strain he puts on them.

The main point is that whatever Mark Roth does to deliver that powerful ball, you may be sure that, at the moment of the explosion point, his body is obeying all the basic fundamentals of good bowling, his body is square to his intended line, his shoulder follows through beautifully, and his head stays down at the line.

You, too, may be unorthodox in some aspects of your bowling style. As you analyze the bowling instructions given in this book, compare what you are doing with the recommended classic bowling style, but do not make radical changes in your style without carefully considering them first. Perhaps you slant a bit on your second step but get back on the straight track with your third and fourth steps. Excellent bowler Marshall Holman is guilty of this fault, but I certainly would not suggest that he change any part of his successful bowling delivery.

Don't be afraid to be unorthodox. Understand the fundamental facts of that moment of final delivery at the foul line—the square body, the follow-through, the bowling arm and hand close to the left side, and the left foot sliding straight forward or slanted counterclockwise, if necessary, in Earl Anthony's extra-lift fashion.

If you find, for example, that you can make the 10-pin more frequently by bowling down the right-hand side of the lane, then by all means do so. Remember, bowling, like golf, is not a game of "how?" but of "how many?"

Here Del Warren shows the unorthodox wrist position of some of the modern-day professional bowlers who crank the ball in their backswing. Mark Roth is a notable example of this type of bowler. This technique requires great physical strength, and since it is a flaw in the delivery it takes great concentration to bring the action off every time in the same way.

Del Warren demonstrates the unusual cocked-wrist delivery featured by several of the leading professional bowlers of today, notably Mark Roth. This type of delivery takes great physical strength and is probably beyond the capability of the ordinary bowler.

14
Gadgets, Gizmos, and Gloves

Sometime in the 1950s a true innovation in bowling equipment and technique emerged—the invention of the bowler's glove. It had become evident that bowlers needed physical support to prevent their wrists from breaking downward from the overpowering weight of the ball when they first placed it into the forward swing. The earliest gloves had a pad that fit between the palm of the bowler's hand and the ball, acting as a cushion that kept the bowler's hand on the side of the ball where he or she wanted it to be.

Later other experiments were made with the bowling glove. Now a great many top bowlers use a glove that gives them firmness, even rigidity, at the wrist. The fact that they continue to bowl with a glove is certainly a good indication that the master bowler should consider using one, too. Be careful to get one that fits your hand exactly. You do not want a glove with any play in it. It may work for you as it does for the stars.

Recently another gadget has appeared on the bowling scene. It is a finger-splint meant to position the right forefinger on the ball in the same place every time and prevent any downward break of the wrist. Try one. It, too, might be of benefit to you.

Some training devices for bowlers are also on the market now. One that seems to have promise as a means to practice your delivery away from the lanes is a harness that fits your bowling arm and hand and has a harness which keeps you from letting go of the ball.

Any or all of the bowling gadgets or gloves may be useful to you. Try them all. They may improve your game.

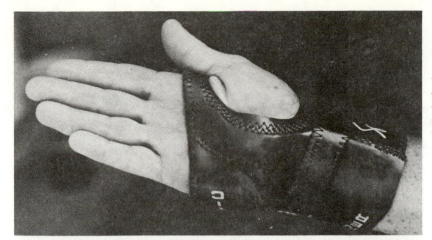

This is a firm wrist accessory that leaves the fingers free. If your hands are tough, you can use it to advantage. Otherwise, you might consider a glove that protects the surface of the fingers from wear.

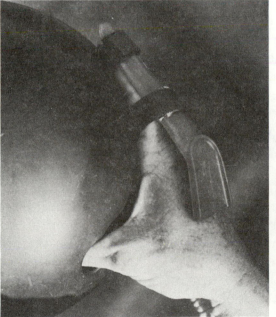

Here is a practice device called "The Bowler's Aid." It is meant to improve the bowler's swing and increase strength. It can be used at home, away from the lanes, as a practice tool.

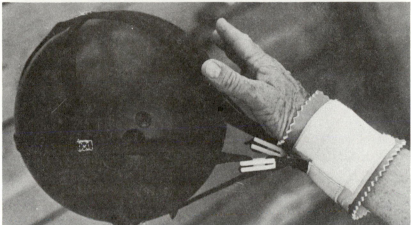

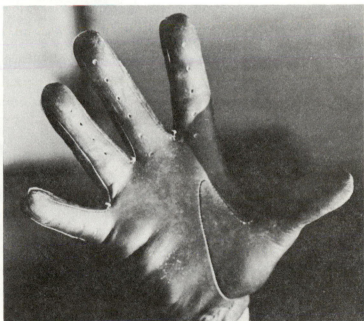

(Left): Here is another gadget, a finger splint that helps the bowler to keep from bending the wrist in the backswing. The curved piece bites into the hand and reminds the bowler of what not to do. *(Right):* Here is another type of bowling glove that you may want to use. It is a skin-tight golf glove with an especially close fit around the base of the thumb. It is expensive and does not last very long, but it prevents a lot of wear on the fingers. Bowlers who bowl many games in succession find it very useful.

15
Exercises for the Bowler

In order to bowl your best at all times, you should be at your highest level of physical fitness. You have made a commitment to excel at bowling. You must also make a commitment to attain the best possible physical condition in order to achieve your goal.

Your body is made up of many different parts, all of which should be brought as close to optimum physical shape as possible. Your body needs to be slim and lean so that you do not find yourself carrying unwanted pounds into the late games of a long series, thus contributing to a weariness that might sap your ability to roll the ball at your usual speed. There is an expression in racing that fits the situation: "I don't care how fast I come out of the chute; I just want to finish first." It is absolutely necessary, therefore, that you examine your stamina, your staying power. And I am sure you will agree that no matter how impressive your stamina is at the present time, it can and should be improved.

If you are overweight, decide how many pounds you need to lose to get into good shape. I recommend that you do this in a sensible fashion by resigning yourself to altering your eating lifestyle for the better, rather than by going on any crash diets. Ask your family physician to give you a balanced diet that will slowly but surely reduce your weight to the level you want to reach. Throughout the diet, resolve to eat carefully, drink moderately if at all, and lead what is called a regular life with a consistent routine of exercise, work, sleep, recreation, serious bowling, and bowling practice. Once your weight is under complete control, resolve to maintain it at that level for the rest of your life.

All good bowlers need strong legs. Your legs, especially the sliding leg, suffer a good deal of shock on every bowling delivery. It is not uncommon for bowlers to feel muscle strain in their legs and, of course, in their arms, shoulders, and back.

The exercise program you develop should

pay particular attention to increasing the tone and strength of the muscles in your hands, arms, legs, shoulders, and back.

JOGGING, WALKING, AND BICYCLING

I recommend that you try a jogging program in order to strengthen your legs and your overall physical condition. Progress gradually, starting with a brisk walk and jogging half a mile or a mile a day, and slowly increase the distance until you can run from two to six miles a day without strain. Watch your pulse rate carefully, day by day, and in a few weeks you will find that your resting pulse rate is getting lower and lower, a most desirable effect because it indicates that your body machinery is working more efficiently.

If you do not like to jog—and many people find it boring, monotonous, even unpleasant—by all means find a substitute exercise that will provide the same results as jogging. Try walking at least two miles a day at a rapid pace and then increase your distance to three or four miles. While walking is not as rigorous an exercise as jogging is, it will give you the final result you seek: better leg power, better wind, and a better overall physical condition.

Another alternative to jogging or walking is bicycling. Find the type of exercise you like and can live with from day to day and indulge in it on a regular basis. Keep a daily chart of your achievements in distance traveled and in elapsed time. Set goals for yourself in distance and time, always striving for better physical condition. If you want to be a champion bowler you must have the body of a champion.

LIFTING WEIGHTS

Jogging, walking, and bicycle riding are all great exercises to improve your overall fitness. In order to concentrate on further localized improvements, such as hand, arm, and leg strength, it is very useful for the serious bowler to exercise with weights. For a modest investment of less than $50 you should be able to outfit yourself with suitable weights for a modest weight-lifting program. In my own case I found that a twenty-pound barbell was a great help to me in strengthening my bowling arm and all the various muscles that come into action in the arm and shoulder in a bowling delivery. I made it my habit to swing the barbell twenty times a day, mentally focusing on steadiness while I performed the exercise. The result was that the sixteen-pound ball felt light after my body became accustomed to the heavier barbell. I recommend that you try using barbells. It may work as well for you as it did for me.

STRETCHING EXERCISES

Suppleness is defined in *Webster's Third International Dictionary* as the ability to move and bend with agility and timeliness. To bowl well you need suppleness as well as strength. Most of us think of stretching exercises when we think of suppleness. As our bodies have matured we have habitually tensed certain muscles in our bodies until

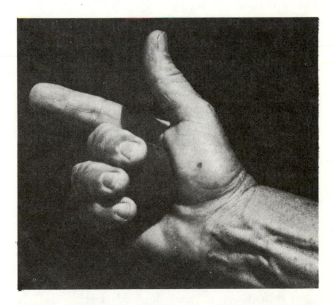

Here's the way to do the rubber ball squeeze as a way of practicing the squeeze technique. With the ball in the palm of your hand and with your fingers relaxed, suddenly clench the third and fourth fingers around the ball and hold tightly for seven seconds.

tension became a way of life for us. Our bodies have become less naturally supple, creating the need for remedial exercises such as stretching to dissolve the tension.

Tension leads to stiff joints, aches and pains, and restricted blood circulation. Stretching exercises will help you lessen the tension in your body and avoid postbowling stiffness in your bowling shoulder, your bowling arm, and your legs.

Stretching exercises should be done in a relaxed manner and carried out intelligently. By no means should you push and pull your body through various extended positions, gritting your teeth in pain. This will hardly relieve your tension. Such a program might lead you to think you are making progress as your body adapts to the daily stretching, but this sort of program actually puts you one step backward every time you take two steps forward. It is a painful approach and sets up inhibiting psychological reactions.

The best way to achieve suppleness is to consider the program as three parts of relaxation and one part of stretching. If you ask your body to become more supple, it will, but you must cajole it. Here are some excellent guidelines on effective ways to urge your body to stretch.

1. You are your own director and stretching expert. You don't need to ask anyone else where and to what degree you need to stretch, because it is your own body, and your own mind inside that body, that will tell you what to do and how far to go without undue strain.

Whenever you feel tight, simply relax into a slightly more extended position than you are used to whenever you feel tight. That may sound too simple, but that's all there is to it. Feel where you are tense—your neck, your shoulders, your legs. Breathe deeply and imagine that your breath is moving out of your lungs and directly into the tight area, where it will loosen the knots of tension.

2. Stretching should be a good feeling, and once you practice it you will find it *is* good. Picture a cat stretching after a nap. Become a human cat, slowly, pleasantly stretching your muscles.

3. Stretch for only three or four minutes at a time and do so twice a day, once in the morning and once in mid-afternoon. Two daily sessions are more effective than is one ten-minute session a day. Remember to be nice to your body. Don't force anything, but stretch smoothly.

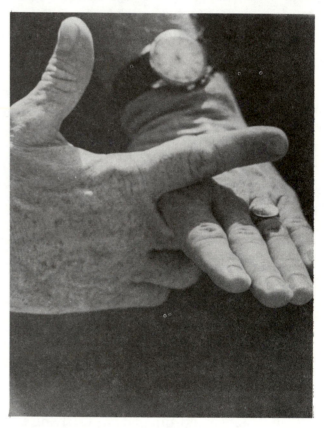

Here is the way to do the bowler's finger press. Press down hard for seven seconds on your third and fourth fingers as you maintain them in the presqueeze position. You can do this exercise a number of times a day, at your work or in your car while waiting for a traffic signal. It is a great exercise for hand and wrist strength.

4. Be sure to stretch when your body is warm, not cold. It's easier, feels better, and does your body more good when you're warm. This might mean that you schedule one of your stretching sessions after a warm

morning bath and the other after an evening shower. You will probably feel that this will lead to more frequent baths, but this will also help you along the road to physical fitness—even bodily perfection. Don't stretch when you are cold. You may pull a muscle and set yourself back until it heals thoroughly enough for you to continue the program.

5. Stretch any way that you feel provides the results you want. Experiment with various moves and find the one you like. Record them mentally or even physically in a notebook and build your own personal set of stretching exercise routines.

ISOMETRIC EXERCISES

Let's talk about isometric exercises. Used regularly, they are a marvelous way to improve your overall physical condition. When specifically directed toward the muscles used in bowling, these exercises will eventually help you improve your bowling.

I highly recommend isometric exercises. In my own situation, I was unable to handle the full fingertip ball because of insufficient finger and wrist strength. After a whole year of studious isometric exercises such as those I describe here, I was able to use the fingertip ball most successfully for the rest of my bowling career.

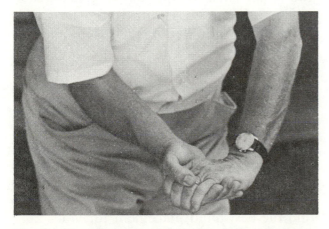

The hand press exercise. Concentrate on your bowling hand and arm. You will be amazed at the increased strength you will achieve if you carry out this exercise every day.

Isometric exercise is defined by *Webster's Third International Dictionary* as exercise that "takes place against resistance without significant shortening of muscle fibers and with marked increase in muscle tone." Isometric muscle contractions, therefore, are those in which the muscles neither shorten nor lengthen, but only contract. In isometric exercises you don't move your joints and you don't move a load. The load involved in the exercises is solid, anchored, steady, or too heavy to move.

A typical exercise done by a weight-lifter is the bench press. The lifter lies on his or her back on a bench, lifting and lowering weights with the arms. Each time he or she lifts and lowers, every joint in the arms and shoulders must be moved by the muscles in order to lift and lower the load. Suppose the weight is immovable. The exerciser exerts the same amount of effort against the weight, but it doesn't move. Only the muscles contract. The joints don't move at all. The harder the weight is pushed, the farther the muscles contract.

The contractions are hard to detect by anyone who might observe you carrying out an isometric exercise program. It is the perfect kind of exercise for you to do wherever you are—in your car, in your office, or while watching television in your living room.

The degree of each muscle contraction is completely at your discretion, and only the muscles you choose to exercise get a workout. The experts tell us that if you can hold a full contraction for seven to ten seconds you will gain strength in that muscle. Furthermore, the experts also believe that a very few isometric exercises per day are required to attain maximum improvement. That makes the exercise program simpler and easier than other exercise programs that require considerably more physical activity, and yet as successful in the final results as any other type.

Isometrics do not replace your regular

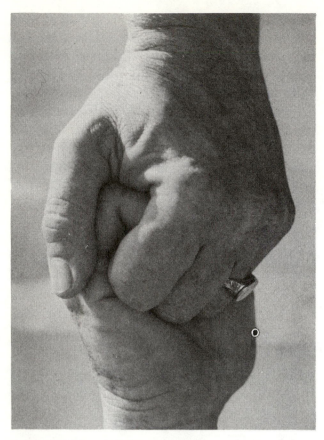

Here's an illustration of the Hooked Finger Pull exercise. This will strengthen your shoulders and upper back if you do it regularly. It should be performed with your fingers together in front of your chest, with your arms a little lower than chest height.

exercise program but should be added to it. Incidentally, you don't have to go through a warm-up procedure for isometrics. You warm up for an isometric exercise just by applying only 50 percent of the muscle contractions you will eventually apply. That's all.

I have broken down the following isometric exercises into two parts. The first part aims at general strengthening of the basic major muscles used in every physical activity. The second part relates to specific muscles required for good bowling performance. Necessarily, some of the exercises overlap in their results and intent.

General Isometrics

The following isometric exercises are meant to be performed in private, in your recreation room or bedroom.

On each of the following recommended isometric exercises, time yourself by counting seconds: "one thousand and one, one thousand and two," and so on, to one thousand and seven, for a total of seven seconds.

The Arm Curl. This exercise is meant to develop and firm the biceps. Clasp your left hand firmly in your right hand, with your palms together. The left arm is extended down and across the body while the right hand is held near the right hip with the elbow flexed slightly. Flex the right arm upward as hard as you can while you apply equal downward pressure with the left hand. Do this both ways—left hand to right, right hand to left—to give both arms a balanced workout.

The Back Arm Lift. This exercise will develop and firm the triceps, the muscles on the back of the arm. Place your left arm behind your back and grasp it tightly with your right wrist. Keeping your right elbow straight, lift your arm up and away from your back as your left arm resists the pull. Alternate arms but emphasize your bowling arm, of course.

The Hooked Finger Pull. This is an excellent exercise to strengthen your shoulders and upper back. Hook your fingers together in front of your chest with your arms a little lower than shoulder height. Pull outward with a steady pull.

The Arm Press. This is the opposite of the Hooked Finger Pull exercise. It will strengthen your chest, back, and shoulder muscles. Join your hands together at a little lower than shoulder height. Push equally hard against both hands to reach maximum pressure and contractions. Be careful not to strain your wrist, however; experiment to find the best hand placement for you.

The Hand Press. Here's a good exercise to strengthen and develop the muscles of the forearm. Holding both hands in front of your body, make a fist with your left hand and insert it between the third and fourth fingers of your right hand. Your right hand fingers should be curved toward you. Press down with the fingers of your right hand while you bring your left fist up to counteract the pressure.

The Shoulder Hugger. This exercise will strengthen your shoulders and back. Cross your arms in front of your body a little above your waist. Give yourself a big hug.

Your bowling ball, bag, and shoes weigh about twenty-five pounds and are excellent to use in strengthening your arm and shoulder muscles. When you swing the bag forward, try to assume the same body position your body would have in a regular delivery. Keep your eye on a spot in front of the arc and concentrate on following through with your arm and shoulder. This is a great exercise and one that will keep you in good trim when you can't get to a lane to practice.

The Shoulder Hugger Squeeze. While doing the Shoulder Hugger exercise, move your arms up to just below your armpits. One arm will have to cross over the other. The top arm should grip the back of the arm that is holding the side of the body. A big squeezing hug will give the muscles in the shoulders and back a real workout.

The Sit-Up V. You don't need to be told how to do this one. Everyone knows how to do it. Sitting on the floor with knees flexed,

raise your trunk about halfway toward your knees and hold that position. Straighten your legs with your toes pointed and lift them from the floor to the same angle that your trunk is making with the floor. Your body will now be in a V position with your buttocks at the base of the V. This is a great exercise for strengthening your abdominal muscles.

The Arm Pushaway. This exercise will strengthen the muscles of the shoulders, back, and arms. Stand in the center of a doorway with your feet wide enough apart to give you a solid base. With your hands at shoulder height, place them against the inside of the door frame and attempt to push the frame apart.

The Leg Push-Apart. This is good for strengthening the upper and lower leg muscles. It is related to the arm pushaway.

Position yourself on the floor so that the area of your lower legs just above your ankles is against either side of a doorway. With your legs spread apart against the door frame, try to spread them farther apart against the resistance of the door frame.

Office Isometrics

Several other isometric exercises can be performed while you are at work, in your car, or in your living room watching TV. In fact, the more you experiment with isometric exercises the more you will come to enjoy using them—and especially enjoy the beneficial results that come from regular use.

The Wastebasket Squeeze. Most of us have a wastebasket near our desks. Keep your basket in front of you, and every time you use the phone put the inside of each foot against the outside of the basket and squeeze. This exercise will strengthen your leg and groin muscles.

The Desk Lift (Hands). Put your hands under your desk and attempt to lift it from the floor. Practice putting your hand in the squeeze position at delivery and lift straight up, applying resistance to the clenched third and fourth fingers of your bowling hand.

The Desk Lift (Legs). While you are sitting in front of your desk, hook your feet under it and attempt to lift it with your ankles. This exercise will strengthen the thigh muscles in the front of the legs.

Ball Squeeze. Keep a rubber ball with you at all times and practice squeezing it, holding it for the seven seconds many times a day. Each time you telephone you should remind yourself to carry out this exercise.

Car Exercises

The Steering Wheel Crusher. To strengthen your arms, chest, and shoulders, use your steering wheel as your resistance point. Try to compress it from the three o'clock and nine o'clock positions. Sit back until your arms are fully extended.

The Steering Wheel Pull. Using the same positions that you did in the Steering Wheel Crusher exercise, try to pull the wheel apart. This is a great exercise for firming the backs of the arms and developing the chest and back muscles.

Here is a great way to exercise and strengthen the hamstring muscles of the legs. Lean against a wall with your arms at shoulder height and gradually move your legs backward away from the wall while you attempt to maintain a straight body position.

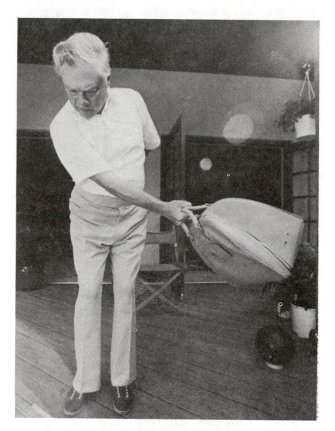

Here is another exercise you can do with your bowling bag as a twenty-five-pound weight. If you swing it slowly in front of you, from right to left, you will free all the muscles in your shoulder and increase the muscle tone of your body as it is forced to turn from side to side. Keep your left arm behind you for best effect.

For greater finger strength it is obviously one of the best exercises a bowler can do. Keep another rubber ball on the seat of your car and do the squeeze at every red light.

The Steering Wheel Bowler Squeeze. As you wait for a traffic light, put your bowling hand into the squeeze position and pull up toward your face on the upper edge of the steering wheel. This exercise will not only improve your hand and wrist strength but will also strengthen your abdominal muscles.

Explosion Point Exercise

I would like to call your attention to one final isometric exercise I have developed for my own use. It is one that I firmly believe will help improve your bowling style more than any other. I call it the Explosion Point isometric exercise, and if it worked for me it should work for you.

Here's how to perform it. Place yourself in a doorway (or up against a wall) so that the edge of the door is opposing your right hand and arm. Put your left foot in a straight sliding position at the door sill and put your entire right arm, right hand, and wrist up against the right-hand side of the door.

Keep your hand in the squeeze position and push against the door, making sure that the line from your fingers to your shoulders is perfectly parallel to the floor, and also that your body is squared to the imaginary bowling line. Your hand and wrist should be close to your sliding foot. You should have a feeling of squareness to your line. You are rehearsing the perfect bowling delivery position.

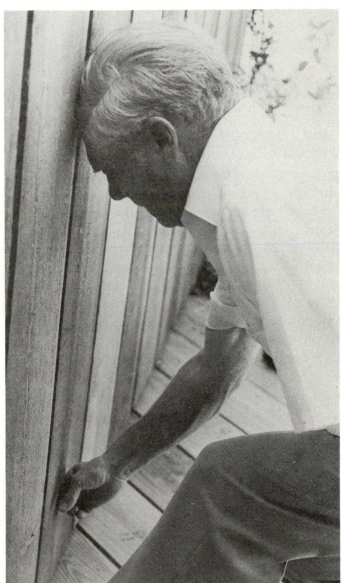

Here is a way to practice the isometric exercise of the action of lift at the line. Assume the bowling delivery position and press forward with your hand clenched in the pre-squeeze position. Hold the position for seven seconds. This exercise also strengthens the forearm and shoulder. You should do it every day.

16
The Mental Side of Bowling

HOW TO PSYCH YOURSELF INTO WINNING

I cannot overemphasize the importance of the mental side of bowling. I am certain that you have seen many bowlers' games collapse completely when they have come under pressure in the ninth and tenth frames of an important match game. Suddenly, the smooth delivery becomes jerky and hurried. A simple one-pin spare is missed, one that under normal conditions the bowler would have made every time.

What happens in the bowler's mind when he or she is under pressure? I can tell you because I have been there hundreds of times. There is a sudden awareness of many insignificant little things that normally would not distract you but do now. You are aware of the mannerisms of the other bowlers, what is happening a couple of lanes away. It seems that your mind wants to think of anything but what it should really be concentrating on, namely, getting the next frame filled—with a strike, if possible.

In order to be able to concentrate as completely as possible under pressure conditions, it is necessary for you to practice bowling under pressure. For example, you must simulate the pressure situation even when you are practicing alone. You can do it this way. When you are rolling a practice game alone and are in the early frames of the game, imagine that you have an opponent bowling a frame ahead of you and that he is a double ahead of you all the way.

That thought will put pressure on you to get your own double or triple and catch up to your ghost opponent.

Then, beginning with your sixth and seventh frames, start mentally talking to yourself about how you must go all the way with strikes to finish the game and beat your imaginary opponent. Your dialogue might sound something like this: "This guy (your imaginary opponent, that is) is not going to miss and he may even get nothing but strikes from now on. I have to strike in every frame."

As you practice this sort of personal pep

talks provoking yourself into a winning state of mind and ability, you will find that you do not always succeed in getting those important strikes. But you will find that sometimes you do manage to perform well under your own manufactured pressure. Then you will begin to understand your odds, that is, the percentage of times that you do perform well and get the strikes that finish in a winning game.

At first you may perform well one time out of five. You should not be surprised if you find that is an average beginning percentage for you. Then, as you continue your pressure practice, and as your overall bowling ability increases in its effectiveness, you will discover that your success-under-pressure percentage will begin to rise. You should be able to bring it well above the 50 percent mark, to 60- or even 70-percent effectiveness.

Can you expect perfection? There are always certain unknowns that come into play during the last few frames of a bowling match. Remember, your opponent is psyching himself, too, and sometimes no matter how well you score, he manages to get one pin more and win. Pure luck plays a large part in a big score. One pin that rolls loose and breaks up or does not break up a devastating split in the middle of a string of strikes, one bad rack with the 5-pin slightly off center, one spare made the wrong way by a pin bouncing off the kickback or sideboards—all these things must be accepted as part of the psychology of winning and losing gracefully.

Practicing pressure bowling alone is necessary, but you must also seek out opportunities for pressure bowling in so-called pot games and, of course, in as many bowling tournaments as you can conveniently enter. Some of the roughest, toughest pressure in all bowling occurs in such famous bowling tournaments as the Peterson Classic, which has been held in Chicago, Illinois, for years. This tournament, for individual bowlers, is famous for its slick oiled lanes and bowling pins of mixed weights. Furthermore, the lanes are not oiled in a consistent manner but are left with patches of dry spots. It takes an extremely skillful bowler, or perhaps I should say an extremely lucky bowler, to bowl well at the Peterson.

Other similar tournaments are good proving grounds for pressure bowling. The thought of $10,000 awaiting a long string of strikes will put fear into the hearts of nearly every bowler. All you can do is fall back on your experience and knowledge and avoid letting the pressure disrupt your concentration. Roll your own game. Keep your rhythm. Don't change your style unless you are certain you have to do so. In conclusion, my advice is: learn to bowl under pressure!

Competence is demonstrated and success is determined by the constant application of the best solution to the problems of the game, the correct decision, the correct adjustment again and again. The great competitors, the truly competent, the master bowlers never let up. They see every game, every action in that game, as significant to them and worthy of their concentrated effort.

Few bowlers reach the level of mental maturity necessary to attain complete mastery of themselves and their games. But all bowlers can and should analyze their own behavior and performance, especially under pressure, recognize their failings, and pinpoint any conduct that is inconsistent with the desire to attain competence. They should look particularly closely at repetitive failure, which is usually a sign that further physical practice or mental concentration directed toward a particular phase of the game is needed. They should review and reconsider the feelings and mannerisms they exhibited while failing. They should record these experiences to see whether they form a pattern. For instance, a bowler might note that, after missing a 10-pin, he or she often rolls a careless first ball in the next frame.

That pattern might be changed by resolving not to become angry about a miss and through determination to work harder on making the 10-pin.

Here are some thoughts on developing a winning attitude in bowling. You might call these a champion bowler's credo.

1. I will recognize that there is a difference between the game of bowling and the real world. Whether I deserve to win and to excel has nothing to do with my performance. I must perform in the best possible form at all times and seize the opportunity for myself, whether I deserve it or not.

2. I will recognize my own motivations and intentions and keep my mind fixed clearly on the long-range target I have in mind, on complete personal control over the game, or on bowling from both the physical and mental side of the sport.

3. I will remain self-assured and continue to believe in myself in spite of pressure, failure, embarrassment, or the superior skill and/or luck of my opponent.

4. I will attempt to forget past failures. I will ignore distractions along the way.

5. I will be a champion bowler, or if not a champion bowler, I intend to excel at the game to the very best of my ability.

Recently, one of the greatest bowlers of all time was bowling in the final game of a professional bowler's tournament, which meant a great deal of money and the prestige of an important title were at stake. His opponent got several lucky hits in the early frames of the game after the star had been hitting the pocket hard and beautifully solid, but not carrying the 10-pin. After another "lucky" double by his opponent, the star missed a simple 10-pin spare to fall moderately behind in the score. He still had time to win the game, if he could pile up a few strikes of his own while his opponent stopped striking or even suffered a miss or split. Amazingly, the star blew a second 10-pin and thus lost the game and title. Oddly

enough, his opponent did falter, but by then it was too late for the star to do anything about it. The moral of this story might well be that no matter how great a bowler's reputation may be, he or she remains human and subject to loss of mental equilibrium when faced with the capricious luck of the game.

If we could control our bodies perfectly all the time, there would be no need to test ourselves through sports. Competition is a test of self-control. We are excited by the opportunity to test our ability to control our emotions, our bodies, our ability to perform satisfactorily or even substantially well under pressure. Coming down to the tenth frame, the bowler who is best controlled usually wins.

It is not easy to find a solution to a psychological problem. The first step is to recognize one when it arises. Just as improvement in physical skill is attained through regimented practice, so should psychological improvement be attempted in an organized fashion. Failure is to be expected sometimes, but ultimately you will see progress. The reward—in winning, in competence, and in sheer joy at having conquered the problem—will be well worth the effort you put into it.

Here are some tips on recognizing tension in yourself.

1. Watch your breathing. Short, shallow breathing indicates tension. Holding your breath signifies extreme tension.

2. Check for muscle stiffness and aches. These symptoms indicate tightness over long periods of time. The head, neck, shoulder, and upper back are most often involved. Watch for an overly tight grip in your fingers, hunched shoulders, or a clenched jaw.

3. Note your body heat. Overworked nerves create heat. You will perspire more under pressure; sometimes you will even break into a sweat over your whole body.

4. Look out for abnormal fatigue. Anxiety and frustration at not performing as well as you had hoped to do may cause exhaustion or at least deep fatigue.

You can avoid pressure by not competing. You can fall before it or you can thrive on it. We have all heard it said about a particular competitor, "He thrives on pressure!" That is, that individual has learned to control himself, his bodily actions, and his emotions so that the knowledge that he is in control allows him to relax and produce his very best performance.

Unrealistic expectations of achievement invite disappointment and discouragement. Be sure that you set goals for yourself that require gradual step-by-step improvement, one element at a time. If you were missing one 10-pin in five at the start, it would be unrealistic to insist that you stop missing them at all right away. It would be better to set a target of, say, one in ten misses inside a month, one in twenty in two months, and then one miss only rarely from then on.

TAKE YOUR TIME

Famous golfer Walter Hagen boasted that he always "took his time" going through life. He claimed that he even shaved in leisurely fashion in the morning in order to set the proper tempo for his day. I recommend that you also take your time in your everyday life and in your vocation, or avocation, of bowling.

Let's say that you have reached the last frame of a major bowling tournament. The bowling star has just had a resounding, perfect pocket hit, and unfortunately the 10-pin has stubbornly refused to fall. The crowd knows that the 10-pin is an easy spare for a good bowler, but it senses at this dramatic moment that it could be troublesome for the star bowler. He steps up to his starting position a little more hurriedly than he usually does. He hardly sights his target before his footwork starts. He is in a hurry to get the spare over with and, out of rhythm as a result of hurrying, he reaches the line with his body too quickly, dumps his ball at the line, and everyone watches in horror as the ball falls off into the channel for an irrevocable and foolish miss.

What happened? The star bowler did not take his time as he usually would do. What is the lesson to be learned? It is obvious: it is necessary that you take your time on every ball rolled, on the first strike ball or the second spare ball, for frame after frame after frame.

It is very important that early in your bowling career you analyze the type of person you are and work out your general timing routine accordingly. If you are a slow, deliberate person, you should bowl in a slow, deliberate fashion. If you are a quick-tempered, fast-moving individual, you should plan a fairly rapid bowling routine. If your nature lies somewhere between slow and rapid, you should try to work out a routine in keeping with the normal tempo of your life. From the moment you awake in the morning until you have finished your last frame, constantly keep in mind the thought that you will take your time today, be deliberate about everything you do.

Let's say that you are going to bowl on an early afternoon shift. You might plan to sleep for an extra hour or two in the morning to get some additional rest. Have a leisurely breakfast and then start thinking about how you will bowl that day. See yourself in complete control of your emotions, in complete management of your body and bowling style. Keep saying to yourself, "I will take my time. Nothing will hurry me. I will let nothing bother me."

Allow at least an hour of extra time for any emergency that may arise. Your car might break down. There might be a monstrous traffic jam on the expressway on your way to the lanes. Then, if you do encounter an unexpected delay, you will find that you are mentally prepared for it and, knowing you are, you will remain relaxed about it.

At the lanes, proceed to the locker room to dress, and, once again, take your time. Tie your shoelaces carefully. Double-tie them as you say to yourself, "See how deliberate I am? How careful I am? Nothing will hurry me today." Be conscious of your breathing rhythm. Take deep breaths and exhale even more deeply and more completely than usual.

All the while, keep saying to yourself, "See how relaxed I am? Watch me breathe slowly and deliberately."

Proceed unhurriedly to your assigned lane. This is the time for quiet thinking and deliberation. Although your fellow bowlers are around you now, this is not the time for small talk with your friends. Try to retreat mentally into your own little cocoon. You are already thinking about that very important first ball. You want it to be as good a bowling delivery as you have ever made. You are gearing your mind and body for the snap of authority that will give you your first strike and possibly the first strike of twelve in a row that will give you a perfect bowling game.

As you roll a few shadow balls in practice, you continue to think of deliberateness, of taking your time, of not rushing any of your movements, especially your approach to the foul line. You are careful to observe the action of your practice balls at the pocket, and you can already see that your usual bowling line seems to be working for you.

The lights go on, the pin setters are all sent down at the same time, and the bowling session is on. You are ready, psychologically and physically, because you have been taking your time.

THE LUCK OF BOWLING

As in any sport, there is a considerable element of luck in bowling. The way the pins act after being struck by the ball, or how one pin will react after being hit by another pin, is usually predictable. But then, suddenly, the pin or the ball does something unpredictable. Since bowling pins are no longer made of solid maple as they once were and are now coated with a plastic covering, bowling pins react in an inconsistent fashion these days. In the early days of bowling, the pins flew almost consistently in a single horizontal plane, knocking down any and all pins in their path. Now, however, it seems as if the ball gets down under the modern plastic pin in some strange way and causes it to fly up and over the other pins. The result, of course, is a pin left standing that would have been counted as downed in the old days.

There is some argument that livelier pins give the bowlers more for their money, providing extra thrills in seeing the pins fly across the lane and bounce off the sideboards or kickback. But, as far as the luck of bowling goes, bowlers must be aware that sometimes no matter how perfectly they roll the strike ball, they may not get a strike count. Bad luck will stop them. On the other hand, they must also be aware that a less skilled bowler may sometimes just tick the headpin and, by some strange quirk of luck, start all the pins rotating and tumbling so that when the smoke settles, every pin is down, some of them still spinning on the pin deck.

You must learn to accept your luck with equanimity, which *Webster's Third International Dictionary* defines as "keenness of mental dispositions, emotional balance, especially under stress." *Webster's* then adds this note: "Equanimity suggests a habitual or constitutional emotional balance or poise that is disturbed only by the most trying of circumstances."

Theoretically, the luck of bowling evens out, they say. I, personally, do not believe that it does. I have observed hundreds of good bowlers for many years and have come to the conclusion that some bowlers have more luck than others. I believe that a large portion of good luck in bowling comes as a result of rolling the ball with authority, with snap, and with moderately good speed, but with enthusiasm.

There seems to be an aura of life about the bowling ball of a bowler who is experiencing a lucky streak of strikes. The pins dance and spin on the slightest hit, and that lucky pin comes across the lane at the last moment to spill the standing 10-pin or 7-pin.

I wish I could give you advice on how to be lucky in bowling. All I can say is that, in my opinion, you create your own luck through the liveliness of the ball you roll. The moral is: act alive and bowl with zip, with snap, with authority. The pins will recognize your ball when it hits them, and I guarantee that you will bowl with good luck behind you!

EMOTIONAL CONTROL

I was fortunate to know ABC champion bowler, George Young, who died an early death of cancer. There was never a finer gentleman in bowling, and it was a pleasure to watch him bowl under pressure in the team championships of the 1950s. One time when George needed a strike in a late frame, he was on the way to the line in the middle of his delivery when a fan yelled at him from the crowd, "Aw, go on and throw it, George!" George heard the remark and realized that he was being distracted from concentrating on his target. In the midst of his move to the line, George was able to haul up, that is, to stop the ball in motion before he let it go out over the foul line.

George stepped back to the seats with his bowling ball in his hand, completely ignored the heckler, and slowly proceeded to make his customary timed delivery. He got the strike he wanted, too, and the team went on to victory over the Kathryn team of Chicago, with its famous Ned Day and Buddy Bomar combination.

Later, I talked to George about his remarkable control. He told me that he had practiced that heckler situation many times in the past. He said that he had had a friend act as the imaginary heckler in order to simulate the situation that might arise someday during a tournament. He said that he even had his friend use pots and pans to make terrible noises as he bowled so that he could get accustomed to such an event. He said that it took quite a bit of dexterity to halt delivery while in full motion, but that every good bowler should learn to do so for ultimate control over delivery.

I took George's advice and practiced stopping my bowling swing in midair the way he did. One time, many years later, the trick came in very handy. I was bowling in an Interclub event at the Cleveland Athletic Club, and the crowd was so large that seats had been put on the lanes themselves. It was quite an unusual feeling to bowl between the walls of spectators lining the two lanes in play. I needed a critical strike in my tenth frame, and just as I began my delivery a spectator stood up at a position midway between the foul line and the pins and started to walk toward me. I recognized the distraction and was able to stop my motion before I delivered the ball. Then, having settled down a bit emotionally and waiting until the spectator left my view, I was able to regain my composure and come through with the strike I needed.

The conclusion that should be drawn here is that the master bowler must be in constant control of the bowling delivery, physically and mentally. With control comes self-confidence that leads to superior performance on the lanes. It is well worth striving for.

RELAXATION

Obviously, when you are required to bowl under stressful conditions, you may find that you become tense and that your usual free arm swing becomes restricted. Your whole torso, neck, and back may experience the feeling of tension, especially in your shoulders.

The stressful conditions that cause a bowler to become tense may vary from the few final frames of a twenty-five-cent neighborhood pot game with other friendly bowlers to every frame of an important sweepstakes tournament for a large cash prize. Certainly the ABC tournament ranks highest of all as a tension producer for bowlers, because every bowler wants to bowl his or her very best there, and join the coveted ranks of ABC champions in bowling history.

So it is most important that you learn to control your stress in bowling. I assure you that when you do, you will have another weapon in your bowling armament, one that may give you a victory over a bowler who boasts comparable technical ability, but one who has less mental and emotional control than you.

I highly recommend that every bowler who truly wishes to become a master bowler adopt certain methods of self-hypnosis in order to learn how to relax under pressure.

First, you must discipline yourself by making a firm commitment that you will carry out certain relaxation procedures regularly and faithfully.

You need to convince yourself that if you do work hard to achieve perfection in relaxation, you will prosper in several ways: your score will improve, sometimes dramatically, and you will be personally happier with yourself as master over your body, your mind, and your emotions.

Once you have convinced yourself of these future benefits, you should start to keep a written diary in which you can register your thoughts, your progress, and your lack of progress as you go along.

Now for the relaxation procedures I rec-

ommend. The following is what I call the Regular Relaxation Routine. Every day you must practice twice a day for about ten minutes at a time. One of your practice sessions should be held in the evening, and you will find that a pleasant by-product of it is that you will fall asleep more easily than you ever have. It is very important that you follow the relaxation methods in their proper order. However, when I suggest that you use certain words or phrases, I only intend to give some examples that you might use. You will find yourself developing your own inner dialogue, and once you do, it will be yours alone. When you are concentrating on relaxing your arms, it would not make any difference, for instance, whether you say to yourself, "Now I am going to release all the muscular tension in my forearms" or "Now I am going to relax the muscles in my arm." You might even find yourself mentally talking to your muscles, saying, for instance, "Biceps, you are too tense. I want you to relax now; loosen up."

Before you start your relaxation exercise, you should find a quiet, comfortable place in your house or office where you know no one will disturb you for the ten minutes you need. You may sit down or, even better, lie down. Make yourself as comfortable as you possibly can. Take off your glasses, or remove your contact lenses if you wear them, loosen your tie and belt, take off your shoes, and loosen any restricting undergarments you are wearing. Most important, get into a relaxed, comfortable position before you begin exercising. Let your hands and arms drop to your sides. You are ready to begin.

1. Eyes Closed

Now close your eyes and begin taking deep breaths, inhaling and exhaling deeply and slowly. You may want to count to yourself the number of seconds you take between breaths. I have found that a count of ten suits me. You may find a shorter or longer interval works for you. Try to be conscious of your breathing throughout the whole ten-minute session. You will discover that as you exhale slowly, your overall bodily relaxation will become deeper.

2. Clench and Unclench

Do the second exercise while continuing the deep breathing. Clench both of your fists. Close them and then squeeze them tighter and tighter. As you do, be aware of the tension in your forearms, your hands, and your fingers. Then let go. Relax your hands. Let your fingers become loose. You will notice a pleasant feeling of weariness as the tension goes away.

Feel how heavy your arms and hands are as they rest on your chair or sofa. Next, clench and relax both fists once again. Squeeze them hard, hold the tight fists for a few seconds and then let go once more and relax completely.

As you begin to practice these exercises, you may feel that it is useful to clench and unclench your hands and arms as many as five times. Later, as your exercises start to show that you are improving your ability to relax, you may reduce the number of clenchings to three or increase it to seven or eight. Remember, you will eventually work with your own personal relaxation program, one that you know works for you.

3. The Biceps Relaxer

Now bend your elbows toward you, clench your fists, and contract your biceps muscles in your upper arm. Squeeze them hard and, while you are holding the tension, study the feeling of tightness. Then suddenly let go again. You may do this exercise one arm at a time, or both together, as you wish. Unclench your elbows, relax your hands, and drop your arms forward to relax the biceps muscles. Put your arms once more in their comfortable beginning positions at the side of your body. Consider how your arms feel as you let them go; competely relax them.

4. The Upper Arm Relaxer

Straighten your arms and flex the biceps muscles in the back of your upper arms. Hold them tense for a few seconds, increase the tension as much as you can, and squeeze hard while you study the tension. Then, once more, consciously let go. Relax, return your arms to a comfortable position, and enjoy your release from the tension. Try to feel the depth of your release. Picture a big rubber band that has been stretched to its limit and is now lying completely limp, curled up, unextended in any way.

5. The Facial Relaxer

Clench your jaws and feel the muscles in your face and neck tighten. Again, consider the tension you are introducing into your body. Clench your teeth tighter and tighter. Make a face! Then relax your jaws. Open your mouth and let your lower jaw hang by itself. Feel your facial and neck muscles loosen. Feel the relief from tension.

17
Avoiding Injury

There are many ways in which the bowler can be injured. Some of them are so subtly dangerous that the normal individual would hardly be aware of them in everyday life, yet a muscle pull once suffered by a bowler may remain with him for the rest of his life, haunting him, distracting him, and preventing him from ever attaining his greatest bowling potential.

I would like to relate to you a personal experience that tells how I suffered an unnecessary injury that bothers me to this day. I was bowling in a league in Detroit at a bowling lane with a rear parking lot. The owners thought that, in order to make it easier for the bowlers to enter in inclement weather, they would put an entrance at the back of the lanes. The bowlers entered alongside the end lane.

One stormy night a great deal of water had been tracked in on the passageway next to the lane where I was scheduled to bowl. I arrived early enough to have a practice game and, as I usually do, I checked the

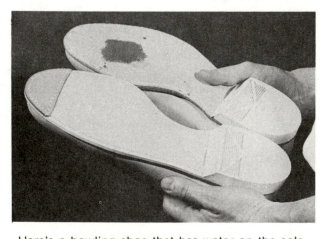

Here's a bowling shoe that has water on the sole, which is very dangerous because it will act as a brake on the lane without the bowler's awareness. Be sure to check your sliding shoe sole frequently to make sure you haven't picked up some foreign substance. Always rehearse your slide on the front of the approach before you make your delivery.

slickness of my normal approach. The lanes were fine; my sliding foot was not sticking. I proceeded to bowl my first frame and left a 10-pin.

When I went to convert the 10-pin, bowling from the far left side of the lane, I did not notice a large wet patch on the approach. I bowled and tripped as if I had been caught by a wire. My body pitched forward and, as I fell, my left foot was turned back under me, my left big toe was twisted upward, and the tendons were torn.

I did not bowl for three weeks and, even now, years later, if I slip and fall, I aggravate that old wound and recall my stupidity in not checking out the conditions of that lane ahead of time.

The first rule for safe bowling is to watch out for water or any other liquid on the lane or around the approaches, which can be hazardous to your bowling delivery. The sole of your left foot is your sliding foot, and the least bit of moisture will cause that shoe to stick on the approach, certainly interrupting the smoothness of your delivery even if it does not cause you to fall and hurt yourself.

that you not leave the lanes at all for fear of picking up water on your shoes. It is usually necessary for most of us to use the toilet at least once during a bowling session. A good tip for you to observe is to touch only the heel of your left shoe to the floor when you walk. You may feel silly, but you definitely won't pick up water on your shoe.

Another problem with getting water on your sliding shoe is that once it is there, it is very difficult to get rid of it. You need to use talcum on the sole to dry it out, and the least bit of extra talcum may cause you to slide too much at the line, substituting one problem for another.

Always test your sliding foot on the lane before you bowl any frame. When you first bowl on a lane, make a mock delivery without a ball to check the slipperiness of the lane. After my unfortunate experience with the left-hand side of the lane, I always make

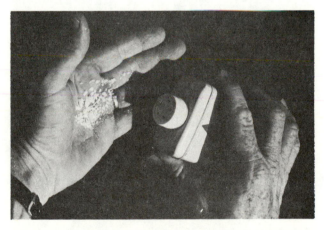

Every bowler should carry a small box of talcum powder for use in case of encountering sticky approaches or getting water on the sliding shoe. You must be very careful not to apply too much talcum. Always put a little bit in the palm of the hand and then apply it. In that way you can control the amount used.

So, monitor the condition of the sole of your sliding foot. Check it physically after you have used a drinking fountain. Watch out for spills of drinks around the scoring table.

In general, in stormy weather it is best

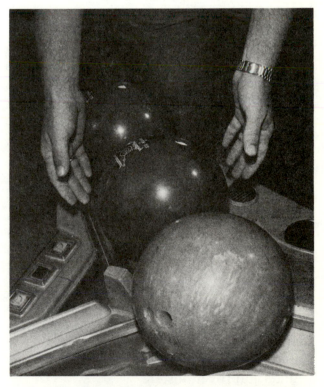

Here's the way to pick up your bowling ball from the return rack so that you will never pinch your fingers between the balls. Always pick it up with both hands from the sides of the rack.

it a habit to check the left side of the lane as well as the normal approach line. I recommend this practice to all bowlers. It may spare you from a nasty injury some day.

Bowlers are often subject to muscle pulls while bowling. You should be careful not to let such an accident happen to you. The bowling ball, bag, and shoes weigh twenty pounds or more, and that is enough weight to cause a muscle pull unless you take care with the way you handle that weight.

Most bowlers carry their equipment in their cars, sometimes on a back seat, but more often in the trunk of the car. So, when you lift your bowling bag out of your car, be careful not to put too much strain on your back or arms. Try to lift it toward you and under you before you lift it upward and out. If the bag is stuck for any reason, do not give it a sudden pull to free it. You may pull the muscle in your upper shoulder if you do.

On the lanes, watch out that you don't catch your fingers between the moving balls on the ball-return rack. The photo shows the proper and improper ways to retrieve a ball from the rack. Always pick the ball up from the side, using both hands to do it. In that way you can't get your fingers smashed between the two balls, and you will distribute the weight of the ball evenly between both of your arms.

Bowlers' fingers are subject to blisters. They, too, can be an annoying and upsetting problem. The skin of the finger starts to feel hot and then starts to work loose and form a blister. If the bowler consistently works a blister on one particular finger at the same place, it is an indication of a badly fitted ball. There should be no squeezing in the ball holes by any one of the fingers. It is believed that the effort of squeezing causes the bunching of the skin layers and lays the foundation for a blister.

If you start to develop a hot spot on one of your fingers, or you know that you are particularly susceptible to blisters in a certain place, you should lubricate that area of skin with petroleum jelly before you begin to bowl. You can also protect such areas in advance by using a protective covering such as the trademarked "Nu-Skin," which puts a clear plasticlike covering on the skin and thus takes the wear off the finger, preventing the blister from developing. If you develop a blister, you must not pick at it. You

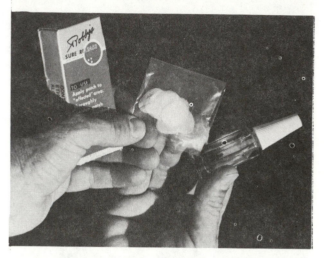

This is a typical repair kit, which every bowler should have and learn to use properly. The basis is collodion, a viscous liquid that hardens and leaves a protective coating on the finger. The little white pads provide a foundation to strengthen the repair.

might slow the healing process by exposing new skin underneath it before it is ready, or worse, you may easily contract an infection that has the potential to get into the bloodstream and cause serious trouble.

The upper limit of the bowler's body consists of the shoulder, upper arm, forearm, wrist, and hand. The motions of bowling take place in the fingers, the shoulder joint, the elbow joint, and the wrist joint. All of these areas are subject to strain and damage. The key to avoiding injuries is to strengthen the muscles involved and to bowl with proper form so that no undue strain is put on the joints.

Shoulder strain is often experienced by bowlers. The muscle tendon units of the

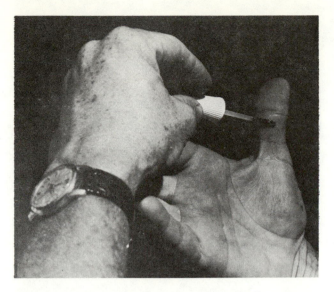

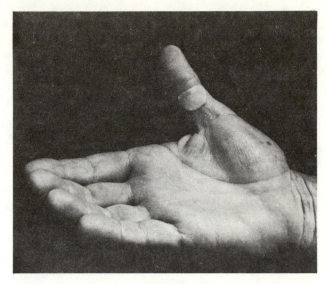

Here is the first step in putting on collodion as a finger protection. The finger must be very dry. Then a first coating of the liquid is spread evenly on the finger, covering a considerably larger area than the sore spot itself.

Here is the way the finger protection of collodion works. The little pad is put on the finger and moistened with the liquid. After it has dried well and hardened, an extra coating of collodion is applied.

upper arm are affected and the result is painful tendonitis and what is called tenosynovitis, inflammation of the tendon sheath. The tendon of the biceps muscle is a frequent site of this kind of muscle-tendon irritation. The front of the upper arm aches and becomes hard to move. There is likely to be tenderness at a particular point in the top front of the upper arm as well. What has happened is that the rotation motion from throwing the ball too hard has irritated the tendon of the biceps. The treatment is complete rest for one or two weeks

with daily heat treatments. Then the bowler should work on special exercises to rehabilitate the shoulder in order to prevent recurrence of the injury. Swinging the bowling bag gently across the body is especially recommended for quick recovery.

If you have suffered this type of injury, once you have returned to bowling, you should be very careful not to throw the ball but, rather, let the ball roll itself as a weight being released from the end of your arm and acting like a pendulum.

18
The Bowling Instructor

Every master bowler in the United States has at one time or another sought counsel and instruction from the best bowling teacher available. We cannot observe ourselves properly in the act of bowling, so it is very difficult to uncover and correct our own faults.

In every locality there are many bowling instructors—some good, some bad, some outstandingly good and successful in bringing bowlers to the top of their proficiency. The bowling instructor need not be a high-average bowler and often is not. However, this individual does have the ability to analyze a bowler's form and state clearly what that bowler is doing right and wrong in delivering the bowling ball.

I recommend that you make inquiries among the high-average bowlers in your area and ask them to recommend one or more good instructors. You will probably be surprised to find that a number of bowlers will name one particular instructor as the best. Once you have found such a teacher, put yourself completely into his or her hands. Tell the instructor of your ambition

John Ruggerio, captain of the famous Stroh bowling team, instructs Mary Last on the proper way to bend her knee at the line as she delivers the ball.

Bowling instructor John Ruggerio shows Ethel Larson how to keep her wrist firm at the start of her pushaway. John advocates keeping a straight line down the arm through the back of the hand.

John Ruggerio, great bowling instructor, shows Mary Last why she is not getting any action on the ball. With her fingers relaxed at the delivery point, she is not getting any lift on the ball.

to be a master bowler, describe your practice techniques and exercise routines, and let the teacher observe you as you bowl. Then, take the advice given and follow it. The same individual may be the best person to counsel you on the proper ball balance you should have in your three bowling balls for strong, stronger, and strongest action. If he is not, ask for a lead to the best local ball driller.

Obtaining good instruction and the best advice on ball balance should help you become the master bowler you want to be.

19

How to Keep Your Own Bowling Records

It is very important that you keep your own personal bowling records. In fact, unless you do, you can never aspire to be a master bowler. All good bowlers keep track of their scores, splits, strikes, doubles, misses, and conversions of both splits and misses. By doing so, it is possible to gauge your improvement and notice both good and bad trends in your bowling.

Let me suggest a rudimentary system of record keeping that will be easy to adhere to and very profitable in the long run of your thriving bowling career. Get a three-ring binder and fifty or more filler sheets. The binder need not be a big one. As a matter of fact, a medium-sized one is best because you will be carrying it in your bowling bag. We all know that your bag is already as full as it can get holding your shoes, socks, bowling ball, and various medical supplies. Here's the way you should set up your pages for easy record keeping.

Notes: "Arrived as first frame was starting, no warm-up. Hurried first game, one split, one miss, no doubles. Slowed down on second game and ball was moving better. Bowled 2nd arrow until middle of second game when moved left one board. Kept second arrow until start of third game when moved one board left, same line, second arrow, and got string of four. Careless in ninth frame and no foundation.

Lane conditions: Normal at start but running slightly at mid–second game. Must be alert for lane changes before I get nose-hits and splits. Must be aware of tiredness in third game and not slow ball. If anything, roll with more speed."

The above is a brief example of what you can do with your little black book of bowling. You should enter your statistics and keep a diary of your thoughts about your game as soon as you can after your bowling session has ended and your mind is still conscious of the physical and psychological conditions that affected your scoring ability. You can keep your book in a rough condition. Then, a day or so later, I suggest that

DATE	LANES	GAME 1	GAME 2	GAME 3	TOTAL	PREVIOUS TOTAL	AVERAGE
JAN. 1	BOWLMOR 11-12	167	195	223	8560 585 8145	585	180 IN 42 GAMES 181 IN 45 GAMES

O SPLITS	O SPLITS	MISSES	DOUBLES	TOTAL STRIKES
2 3-10 5-6	1 5-7 5-7	2 2-4-5-8 2-4-5-8	5	14

you type your records or make a clean copy for neatness and emphasize the points you made in your diary. As you proceed from game to game, from one bowling lane to another, you will begin to build a body of knowledge about your bowling that will help you understand your own game better, thus helping you score better in the long run.

For instance, as you keep your records from week to week, it might become apparent that you are in the habit of rolling your worst game at the start of your series, in the middle, or at the end. If you notice a trend toward low scoring in the opening game, it might indicate that you are not warming up sufficiently before you start rolling. This means that you will have to find some way to get more practice before you start. Many leagues allow only a shadow ball or two before the lights go on and the pin setters are put into operation. I have known bowlers who practiced tossing their bowling balls gently to each other from a distance of five or six feet as a substitute warm-up when they could not roll a line or two ahead of time. I will grant you that it is quite a trick to catch a bowling ball in midair, but it can be done if you are not afraid that you will drop it. And, of course, you need a dexterous fellow bowler who will cooperate with you.

If you notice that you have a trend toward lower scoring in your middle game, it might indicate that you are losing concentration or that you are not adjusting as quickly as you should to changing lane conditions. If you note that your last game is regularly your lowest game, it might be a sign that you are either tiring too soon physically or that you are not adjusting to the changing lane conditions. If you know that fatigue is causing the problem, you will have to go to work on your physical condition to build up your strength and stamina.

The records you keep of your splits and split conversions will soon show a significant trend. For example, if you note that your wide-open splits are 5–7s and 8–10s, your ball is too weak and is not rolling into the 1–3 pocket strongly enough to get the 5-pin out.

When you keep track of your misses, you should also note which pin or pins remained standing after the miss. In that way you will note trends in your bowling that will indicate clearly where you need the most practice in the future.

Let's look again at the imaginary bowler's score sheet. He has missed two 2–4–5–8 spares and the numbers circled indicate the pins left standing. Once he left the 5-pin and once he left the 8-pin. It is obvious that his misses are inconsistent, with the ball rolling too far to the left and missing the 5-pin one time, then going too far to the right so that the ball never got back to the 8-pin. Several conclusions should be drawn: This bowler is rolling an inconsistent second ball. His trouble might be in varying his action on the ball at delivery point, or in varying his speed or line as he aims for this difficult spare. The final conclusion is that leaving 2–4–5–8 spares frequently is a sign of a weak or inaccurate first ball. Secondly, he is missing the spare both ways, with too weak a second ball or too strong a second ball. He must practice this spare until he makes it regularly every time with a strong ball that comes in from the right, hitting the 2-pin on its left side and then carrying on through the pin cluster to take out the 8-pin sleeper.

Your little black book will be invaluable to you as you build several years or more of personal bowling records. You will find that as you progress up the ladder of excellence to true mastery of the game, you will be more and more conscious of lane conditions and the way they affect your scores, favorably or unfavorably.

Some lanes become known as high-scoring lanes and bowlers look forward to bowling on them. Others are known as tough or rock piles. These lanes are often excessively dirty and usually not as well prepared as the better lanes. Most bowlers dread bowling on difficult lanes because it seems that no matter how well you bowl, you never carry the strikes you feel you are entitled to carry and would carry under normal conditions. There are individually difficult pairs of lanes within bowling establishments, as well, and bowlers come to know which ones they are. Many an unexplained absence in league bowling can be laid to the bowler's knowledge that he had to face difficult conditions that night and wanted to dodge them.

The explanation for tough pairs is that sometimes there is a spot near the pocket that has harder wood than the rest of the boards; the board causes the ball to slide rather than act normally in its hooking action toward the pocket. The result is that the final action of the ball is different from what the bowler expects to happen. He might miss the headpin entirely or leave a one-pin spare under circumstances that usually would have brought him a strike.

With your little black book you will be able to anticipate problems with difficult pairs and look forward to the so-called easy pairs. Since psychological preparation accounts for from 75 to 90 percent of bowling success, you will be the master of your bowling fate when you hit a tough pair of lanes. You will have noted that in order to hit lane number twelve, it was necessary in your last encounter with the pair to move several boards to the right on your approach and roll a faster ball to hit high on the headpin, thus counteracting the high board, or slippery spot, in the lane in front of the pocket. Perhaps you will not score as well on the difficult pair as you do on other pairs in the house, but you will pick up a few more spares and strikes than would another unprepared bowler who fishes for a game or two before finally finding the line and correction that were called for all along.

Here is another fact you must be aware of: Bowling lanes are resurfaced at regular intervals. They are sanded until they are as close to being absolutely flat as possible according to American Bowling Congress standards—forty thousandths of an inch from channel to channel. The result is that your carefully assembled information about the way the lanes behave in a particular bowling establishment may suddenly be out of date and invalid. Not until the resurfaced lanes have been used for a while will they again exhibit individual characteristics. But eventually they will, and if you are patient and continue to use your little black book, you will finally win out over the lanes. It is well worth the effort to keep your record book. It will give you an edge over the players who don't study the lanes so methodically.

There are several other reasons for keeping your own bowling records. Human beings and machines make arithmetical mistakes. You want to get credit for each and every pin you knock down. You can and should check your pin totals every few weeks with your league secretary to make sure your records and the league's agree. If you can keep your bowling sheets, by all means do so until you know your scores have been entered and totaled correctly. The sheets themselves are the best evidence. Once you know your scores have been recorded properly, you can throw them away or keep them as you wish. Many bowlers keep their best score sheet as a psychological reminder of how well they have bowled in the past and as an incentive for bowling better in the future.

Final advice: Keep an accurate, neat little black book of your scores and a diary of your thoughts about bowling and watch your bowling skill increase day by day!

20 Women's Bowling

The Women's International Bowling Congress reports that there are now more than four million women bowling regularly in U.S. leagues. There are more than 168,000 leagues in all. It is believed that in addition to the league bowlers, there are another 24 million women who bowl once in a while.

There are two professional bowler groups for women, the largest being the Women's Professional Bowlers Association (WPBA), which is the counterpart of the similar men's group. The female master bowler should inquire about this group by writing to the WPBA, 17 Chestnut St., Chicago, IL 60611. There is also a group of female professional bowlers on the West Coast in a nine-state area. It is called the Western Women Professional Bowlers and can be reached by writing 7056 Apperson St., Tujunga, CA 91042.

The female master bowler should certainly plan to join either one of these excellent organizations. In time, it is probable that the prize money will reach the astronomic heights of the men's tour.

Robin Reams, sixteen-year-old bowler, shows excellent form as she delivers her thirteen-pound ball out over the foul line. Robin has been bowling for five years, starting with a ten-pound ball and now carrying a 161 average in her league. She aspires to be a women's professional bowling champion someday!

The size and strength of the woman bowler are not overly important for bowling success. Some of the greatest women bowlers of all time have been small in stature. For example, Sylvia Wene, a great champion, is only four feet ten inches tall.

Women are better balanced than most men and learn to get to the foul line more smoothly. Since most women are not physically as strong as their male counterparts, they must compensate for overall brute strength by learning to bowl with accuracy. Often a sixteen-pound ball is simply too heavy for the ordinary woman to handle comfortably. Therefore she should use a ball in the twelve- to fourteen-pound range at first, and then once she attains some proficiency, gradually increase the weight of her ball by half-pound increments until she reaches the best balance between the weight of the ball and her accuracy of delivery.

Robin Reams demonstrates her starting position, the traditional one with the left foot on the center dot, the arm and ball ready to go down the line between the second and third arrows. Robin rolls a full roller ball weighing thirteen pounds. Her thumb is at eleven o'clock, her fingers at five o'clock as she starts, and she keeps this alignment throughout her delivery until the explosion point, when she imparts the squeeze or lift to her ball.

A woman's arm is constructed differently from a man's and the result is that a free swing of a woman's arm often causes her to roll a straight ball or even a "back-up" ball, one that curves from left to right for the right-handed bowler. The woman bowler usually cannot roll the "big hook" that many strong men are able to develop, but with practice and proper attention to her hand position at the delivery point, she can keep her thumb at the ten o'clock position and perfect a strong short hook ball that will be very effective under all lane conditions.

Women should guard against rolling the ball too slowly and should work to achieve moderate to good speed in order to knock down as many pins as possible. Women should keep in mind that the speed of the delivery, while obviously controlled by the speed of the footwork to the line, is also greatly controlled by the pushaway and backswing. So the woman who needs more speed should concentrate on a good pushaway. The woman bowler should also be careful to keep her wrist and forearm unbroken right through the delivery point and reach out toward her position spot or line on the lanes, "staying with the ball" all through the release. In all other ways the basic fundamentals of bowling are the same for women as they are for men.

(Left): Robin Reams demonstrates perfect balance and bowling form as she delivers this strike ball down the lane. Note her intense concentration on her target and her clenched fingers, indicating that she has imparted the squeeze to her bowling ball. The position of her sliding foot shows that she has adopted the Earl Anthony trick of turning it counterclockwise to get more leverage at the explosion point. (Right): Scott Haefele, seven years old, the nephew of Robin Reams, shows excellent form as he delivers his ten-pound ball over the foul line. Scott has been bowling for two years in an ABC junior bowling program and has a high game of 175. He is determined to be a master bowler someday!

21
Becoming a Professional Bowler

There are now nearly two thousand members of the Men's Professional Bowlers Association (MPBA). They are bowling in thirty-five or more national tournaments each year and also have some eighty-five separate regional tournaments. The prize money on the tour has reached the staggering total of $4 million. The leading money winners take home in excess of $100,000 a year. Recently, the MPBA established a school to help newcomers in the bowling world become members of the group in good standing.

There is also a Women's Professional Association with several hundred members. Their tournaments are less frequent and the prize money at stake is much less than it is on the men's tour.

If you have any desire to become a professional bowler, it is necessary that you first prove that you are a high-average bowler and have good character and reputa-

tion as well. The male bowler who wishes to join the MPBA must submit certified copies of his high league averages. He must have bowled an average of not less than 190 in the two most recent seasons, based on a minimum of sixty-six games per league. The initiation fee is $75. In order to live moderately well while touring from city to city, the new member of the MPBA tour should count on expenses of not less than $500 a week. Some new bowlers obtain sponsors who enter into business contracts with them and provide a weekly living allowance for the bowler in return for a percentage of the winnings.

The MPBA and WPBA dues are lower for regional members. The best advice I can give you is that by all means you should join the MPBA or WPBA as soon as you can, but make your mark on local lanes before you consider going on tour.

Index